SHE
FLIES
BEYOND

SHE FLIES BEYOND

MEMORIES AND HOPES OF WOMEN IN THE ECUMENICAL MOVEMENT

PAULINE WEBB

BOOK SERIES

WCC Publications, Geneva

Cover design: Edwin Hassink

ISBN 2-8254-1105-1

© 1993 WCC Publications, World Council of Churches,
150 route de Ferney, 1211 Geneva 2, Switzerland

No. 56 in the Risk book series

Printed in Switzerland

She comes sailing on the wind,
her wings flashing in the sun;
on a journey just begun
she flies on.

From *In Spirit and in Truth: Hymns and Responses*,
Geneva, WCC, 1991, p. 52.

My thanks are due to the following friends,
old and new,
who shared their stories, dreams and prayers
during the consultation in Geneva,
17-21 September 1992:

Annathaie Abayasekera
Agnes Abuom
Marie Assaad
Jeanne Becher
Marga Bührig
Aiko Carter
Aruna Gnanadason
Margot Kässmann
Judy Monroe
Mercy Amba Oduyoye
Ofelia Ortega
Sun Ai Lee-Park
Barbara Stephens
Louise Tappa
Bertrice Wood
Hildegard Zumach

Table of Contents

Introduction: The Beckoning Spirit

> Always the breath — the wind — of the Spirit is moving. We know it by its effect. We have no need to ask for its authentication. Is it Protestant? Is it Catholic? Where the fruit of the Spirit is apparent, there the Spirit is at work. We should place ourselves in its course that we may be carried by its impulse, even though this leads us to association with strange comrades... For whatever promotes love and joy and peace has its source in that divine love which sent the Son into the world, not to judge the world, but *that the world may be saved through him*.[1]

It is not only young men who see visions and old men who dream dreams. In the autumn of 1992 a group of young and old women were invited to meet in Geneva to share their hopes and their memories of the ecumenical movement. I personally accepted the invitation somewhat reluctantly. I have spent a life-time in committees, reviewing programmes and making plans. Now that I am retired, I felt I could beg relief from long agendas and prepared documents and drafted resolutions.

I confess too that, as a result of years of working in a male-dominated church, I had, like many women of my generation, been conditioned to feel a certain scepticism about meetings that were for women only. I have always passionately believed that the sexes are complementary and that we need the wisdom of both if we are to attain the fullness of our humanity. For years, along with a few other women given positions of responsibility in the male-led church, I had struggled to convince men colleagues of the importance of their learning to listen to feminine insights as well as to their own experience. I had come to realize at the same time that we women need to learn to trust the validity of our own intuition and to follow where the Spirit leads us. For so long we have been hemmed in by male expectations and presuppositions. We need space and time together where we can throw our customary caution to the wind and let our imaginations take wing, towards "new thoughts of God and new hopes of heaven".

To my great joy, the weekend in Geneva for women of different generations proved to be that kind of experience. On my arrival I was delighted to discover that there was no pre-planned agenda on the table, and there were no prepared documents for us to digest. We were not required to draft resolutions nor reach conclusions. Instead, we were invited to engage in a free-ranging discussion of both our past experience and our future expectations of ecumenism. We decided to keep a record of our conversation with the hope that others, reading this account, will continue along the way with us trying to hear what it is that the Spirit may be saying to the churches. This book is based on that record. It is not an official document of the World Council of Churches, nor is it a detailed report of a high-powered consultation. It is simply a personal reflection on a meeting between a few ecumenical veterans and their younger sisters as we came together in the midst of our ecumenical pilgrimage.

Our conversation took flight in the most unexpected way. Perhaps it was the poster on the wall that inspired us. It bore the logo of the Ecumenical Decade of the Churches in Solidarity with Women. It depicts a dove, clearly of female gender, bearing an olive branch and soaring up towards some distant horizon. Now, I confess that I am not fond of pigeons. In my London home they are frequent visitors to my balcony. They have even taken to nesting in my flower-pots, where they remain in permanent residence outside my window throughout the summer. There they call to one another in a monotonous, cooing gurgle, which sounds as though a constant committee meeting were in progress on my window sill.

A dove is different. According to my dictionary, it is a special kind of pigeon. It is both a traveller and a messenger. Making reference to Genesis 8, the *Concise Oxford Dictionary* defines a dove as "a messenger of good

news or peace", a "type of gentleness and innocence". No
wonder she has become a symbol of the Holy Spirit.

No wonder, either, that in the scriptures the Spirit is so
often associated with the female gender. She broods like a
mother over her young; she sweeps like a wind across the
world; she inspires wisdom, like a woman pondering the
word; she groans as in childbirth, longing for the appear-
ance of a new creation. This is a disturbing Spirit, soaring
where she wills, apparently uncontrollable.

It seems no coincidence that the insights of women are
so often regarded as unpredictable, disturbing and even
disruptive of tradition. Throughout the history of the
church attempts have been made to keep women under
control. Yet women have been among the harbingers of
every movement of renewal. They have been and still are
accused of rocking the ecumenical boat, their influence as
threatening as a powerful wind can be, even to veteran
mariners. The present squalls that have blown up in most
parts of the world around the question of women's ordination, for example, are affecting all the churches, and caus-
ing ecumenical upheaval. For those of us who are passionately committed both to the quest for the unity of the church
and to the affirmation of the full ministry of women, this
tension between ecumenism and our obedience to our
spiritual vocation can cause almost unbearable pain. Dr
Margit Sahlin, the first woman priest to be ordained in the
Lutheran Church in Sweden, once told me of a letter she
received saying: "You are another wound in the body of
Christ." Yet Christ bore all those wounds for the sake of
redeeming our whole humanity. And in heaven, where
those wounds are glorified, the communion of saints knows
no distinction between male and female, Jew or Gentile. It
is only the wounded body of Christ that can bring healing to
the whole of our divided community.

The so-called "scandal" (stumbling-block), as some
people regard it, of women's ordination could be
described as the base rather than the tip of an iceberg

xii

which threatens to impede the future progress of the
ecumenical vessel. It raises issues of fundamental importance to the credibility of our witness to the gospel, which
came as good news for women as well as for men. But in
our meeting in Geneva we were not so much concerned
with the question of women's *ordination* as of women's
sub-ordination in almost every area of life. As we are
discovering in many tragic ways in today's world, all
division, whether it be between churches or between
faiths, between races or between sexes, can cost lives.

Discrimination brings violence and death in its train.
But the Holy Spirit promises life as she wings us forward
into a new united humanity, prefigured in the unity of the
one holy, catholic church.

Archbishop Temple once confessed that whenever he
proclaimed his faith in the holy catholic church, he added
under his breath the prayer that one day it might become a
reality. True catholicism would not be limited by bounds
of history or geography, of race or gender. It would
embrace the whole community of faith throughout the
world, those who share the same tradition as well as those
who are being led into new ventures of faith. It would dare
to trust that the Holy Spirit will lead us all, not only into
the haven of a restored unity but also into the heaven of a
new community.

Throughout the centuries there have been Spirit-filled
women soaring beyond the limits that held them captive and
bringing back glimpses of a new order in which men and
women together could enjoy the fresh air of liberation and
exchange the olive branch of reconciliation. I believe it was
the Holy Spirit that sent the thoughts of the women gathered
at our meeting in Geneva winging away beyond the immediate horizons into a wider, more open ecumenical future than
we have yet seen. We had come from different parts of the
world and were from Orthodox, Catholic and Protestant
traditions. A few were ordained ministers of the word and
sacraments, but most of us were laypeople. Some were

trained theologians, others were working out our theology as we walked through life. Some were mothers, all of us were daughters. We shared our stories with one another and we studied the scriptures together. As daughters of the gospel, we dared, in accordance with the promise of Pentecost, to do our share of the prophesying.

We began by reminiscing. Many of us had last met at the Canberra assembly of the World Council of Churches. That assembly had been bold enough to take as its theme an invocation, "Come, Holy Spirit — Renew the Whole Creation". To call on the Holy Spirit to come and renew the whole creation had seemed to me, right from the start, to be taking a great risk. It is like one of those prayers we make which we secretly hope God will grant on our terms, not God's. The Holy Spirit particularly is that Person of the Trinity who seems most unpredictable and has a habit of working in her own way through chaos to order. Our experience at Canberra had not surprisingly been one of some confusion, considerable controversy and occasional moments of sheer inspiration.

As was to be expected, we women took much of our inspiration from the session that had provoked the most lively theological controversy I can remember at an ecumenical gathering. It was the address given by the Asian theologian, Chung Hyun Kyung. Her exposition of the theme, "Come, Holy Spirit" had been presented with powerful charisma in eloquent speech, exquisite dance and symbolic acts drawn from her own traditional Korean culture. She bade us hear the Spirit's cry within all the groaning of the wounded creation, in the weeping of the oppressed, in the wisdom of the ancestors. She called us to enlarge our awareness of the Spirit's activity, far beyond the limited span of our human existence. The Spirit's energy, she claimed, pulsed through all of creation, so that the whole earth was to be seen as "God-infused", "God-breathed". She challenged us to "think like a mountain", centring our concern not on human beings alone but on all aspects of God's creation. When God made the world, she reminded us, it looked good. It had integrity, with the whole of creation responding to the same rhythm. But human beings have divided it up, erected walls of enmity and division, sought to separate body and spirit, emotion and reason, immanence and transcendence, women and men, black and white, poor and rich, the powerless and the powerful. Chung Hyun Kyung called on the assembly to reclaim the energy of the Holy Spirit and to participate in what she called a "political economy of life", breaking down the barriers and building together truly ecumenical communities where all peoples can enjoy justice and the whole creation may be bound together in peace.

Her words provoked controversy, particularly among those who were used to a more academic approach to theology, and who wanted to define the limits within which the workings of the Spirit can be recognized. They spoke gravely of the dangers of syncretism, of imprecision, even of heresy. But the fiery nature of their response indicated to me the very presence of the Spirit within the debate itself.

"Let us welcome the Spirit," Chung Hyun Kyung had said, "letting ourselves go in her wild rhythm of life." It was with those words still ringing in our ears that we women came together some months later and dared to let our thoughts and words take wing even beyond the horizons of the immediate ecumenical future. We invite you to join us in this dove's eve-view as she still flies on, beyond and into another century of God's economy, beckoning us to share in the building of God's one household for the whole earth.

NOTE

[1] William Temple, *Readings in St John's Gospel*, London, Macmillan, 1939.

1. Bewitched by the Future

All cultures are conscious of the visionary power of women. Visionary power is especially present in oppressed cultures, whereby a spirituality of the oppressed becomes possible. These collective memories direct themselves towards a bygone age... they are the expression of a matriarchal subculture, one that has managed to make room for itself within the dominating culture, where it was able to impress itself on eschatological hope. A marginal subculture can therefore be read out of the Old Testament itself... contradicting a patriarchal religion that puts God on the side of everything that is strong and male and witnessing to a different experience of God, one that does not quite fit into the dominating structure of patriarchal piety.[1]

We began with Bible study. Reading the Bible through women's eyes can be a most illuminating experience. It needs X-ray gifts to penetrate through the overlay of traditional, masculine interpretation to the depth of feminine insight that so often lies submerged, anonymous, sometimes totally ignored by male commentators.

We were fortunate in having in the Geneva meeting Margot Kässmann, pastor and leader of studies at the German Evangelical Academy in Hofgeismar. She led our opening devotions by directing our attention to an obscure passage from the first book of Samuel, chapter 28, verses 7-25.

This story used to be referred to as the story of Saul and "the witch of Endor". But more recent commentators use the less contentious word "medium" or the more magical term "necromancer" to describe a woman suspected of having particular psychic gifts, which enabled her to communicate with the dead. The word "witch" has come to evoke a sense of guilt these days, associated as it is with the horrendous stories of the witch-hunts of the sixteenth and seventeenth centuries. But that association in itself is a reminder of how women have been oppressed by men, and suspected of being an evil influence upon them. Women who showed any special gifts of insight or psychic power or even simply of physical beauty often became the victims of medieval witch-hunts. Young women were suspect if they were sexually attractive; older women were suspect if they seemed possessed of extraordinary spiritual perception. As has so often been the case for women, sirens and saints were equally feared.

In her book *The Gospel According to Woman*,[2] Karen Armstrong quotes the fifteenth-century handbook *Malleus Maleficarum* ("The Hammer of Witches") intended to help inquisitors in the investigation of witchcraft. The author, the Dominican Jacob Sprenger, was convinced that witchcraft was pre-eminently a vice of women, who were far more likely to be seduced by it than men. Women, he argued, were essentially perverse creatures, more vulnerable to the suggestions of the devil than men were. And particularly he believed this was so in the realm of sexuality. "All witchcraft comes from carnal lust," writes Sprenger, "which in woman is insatiable." So the sexual charms of women were seen to be a malevolent force, and the very words we still use to describe attractive women — "charming", "enchanting", "glamorous", "bewitching" — were all at one time associated with witchcraft and therefore believed to be essentially evil qualities.

Fear of the power of women over men is more ancient than the medieval suspicion of their sexual attraction. In every culture women are recognized as being the ones who stand at the margin, as it were, between this life and the life beyond it. It is they who give birth, bringing new lives into this world, and it is they who tend the dying, preparing the body for burial. Traditionally, some were suspected of having miraculous powers, being able to communicate with the spirits beyond the grave. It was such a woman, living in the small town of Endor near

Nazareth, whom Saul visited secretly, even though he had himself publicly condemned such soothsayers and mediums (1 Sam. 28:3,9).

It was fear that drove Saul to seek her out. In dread of his enemies the Philistines, he longed for some word of encouragement from his former mentor, Samuel. He had called on God, but had heard no voice in answer to his cry. He had been unable to see visions or discern the prophets or understand the oracles. So he turned to the only person he believed would be able to help him, the woman of Endor.

In our study of the passage, we noted that even though such women, supposedly gifted with miraculous powers, had been banished from the land by Saul's own edict, he knew where to find her when he needed her help. And even though it had become dangerous for the woman to display her psychic gifts in any way, he still expected that secretly she would be willing to risk her life in response to the pleading of a man when she saw how desperate his plight was.

As so often happens in the Bible, the woman is given no name. She is described simply as "a woman with a familiar spirit", literally a woman possessed of Ob, a word meaning a skin bottle, as though she were simply a container for the spirit that possessed her. But in this story she comes to life as a caring human being, prepared to use her gifts in the service of others, however great the cost to herself. Her perception is stronger than her suspicion, and her compassion overcomes her fear. She even seems to be fearful of the power of her own gifts, and yet under the compulsion of human need she can no longer hide them.

So Saul is able at last, through the medium of the woman, to hear the answer to his questions (Saul's name means "one who asks"). In the dialogue between them, she can not only summon up for him the spirit of the past but also enable him to face the reality of what lies ahead, grim though it is. Using her as a medium, the spirit of

Samuel speaks honestly of what the future will hold for Saul at the hand of his enemies. Then the woman, seeing the king's distress, shows a very practical concern. She bids him sit down and prepares a good meal for him!

In this fascinating story, we as women could recognize much of the tension that still strains the dialogue between men and women, in the ecumenical movement as in every other human encounter. It seemed to point up the different ways in which men and women arrive at their understanding of reality. Saul had until this time put his trust in the acknowledged prophet, in his own kingly status and in his nation's material wealth. When these failed him, he turned to the hidden wisdom of the woman, one of the oppressed. She had been banished to the margins of society, her psychic gifts suspected of being subversive of the accepted, rational order. But when even God seemed to be silent the king turned to the outcast to hear the word of the Spirit. Her grasp of the reality of the situation was quite different from his. It was both prophetic and practical, both visionary and down to earth. She helped him to see not only how things were, but what they could become; she could put him in touch with the past, and also make him aware of the need of the present moment, and was able to nourish him with the strength he needed to face the future.

Our study of that particular dialogue between Saul and the woman of Endor underlined for me one of the emphases of contemporary feminist theologians, and one that is vitally important in the whole development of an ecumenical spirit. It stresses the importance of listening to the voice of the oppressed and particularly to the voice of women. Women's ways of knowing are different from men's, but they have too often been dismissed as "old wives' tales", idle gossip, bewitching nonsense. The British theologian Mary Grey, in a lecture to the Societas Oecumenica in Salamanca in August 1992, had some fascinating things to say about ecumenical dialogue seen from a feminist perspective. She quoted Simone Weil's strange observation that "in Shakespeare only the fools tell the truth". In that word "fools" are included all who are ignored by the powerful, whose wisdom goes unheard, who are regarded as beyond the fringes of established society. They have a way of knowing which differs radically from the perception of those who view the world from positions of power and wealth and status. Their logic is born out of their experience on the margins, of the struggle to survive rather than from the wielding of power.

Grey, quoting from the book *The Other Side of Language: A Philosophy of Listening* by Gemma Corrado Fiumara,[3] describes this different kind of logic in the striking phrase "midwife thinking". This implies the risky venture of helping others to give birth and expression to ideas, which may involve loss both to the one giving birth and to what is born. It requires patience, the ability to wait and to listen and to strive in co-operation with the mysterious, creative powers of life and death.

"It is through this 'listening logic'", said Grey, "that we are becoming aware of other ways of knowing, issuing from Christian feminist base communities, 'Woman Church' groups, refuge groups against domestic violence and so on, which I believe have so much to offer ecumenical dialogue."

She went on to describe what such "listening logic" would involve. It recognizes that many oppressed peoples, and particularly women, have been rendered inarticulate through long experience of being unheard, or of being traumatized by suffering. Even the boldest woman can feel intimidated, for example, when her intervention in a debate is liable to be ignored in a group made up mainly of men, because they do not recognize that she has any authority to speak. Women who have lost all self-esteem through the indignity meted out to them in either physical or verbal abuse shrink from any effort to give expression to their experience. A "listening logic" means listening sensitively enough to enable the other person to put her thoughts into words. It means making the attempt to hear not only the words but also the feeling underlying them and the body language accompanying them which are such integral parts of our communication with one another. Sarah Ruddick has called this kind of listening "maternal thinking", a phase which, it seems to me, graphically describes the gracious way in which the woman of Endor responds to the king and in which he, in his need, learns to listen to her and through her to the words of the prophet.

Listening, responding and acknowledging one another's truth ought to be the basis of all truly ecumenical dialogue. Through it, we would be led to repent of our separation from one another. No longer would we be obsessed by the past or bewitched by the future. We would be released from our fears into a partnership in which we nourish one another in a mutual, ecumenical ministry.

NOTES

[1] Elizabeth Moltmann-Wendel, *Humanity in God*, London, SCM, 1983, p.43.
[2] London, Elm Tree Books, 1986, p.94.
[3] London, Routledge, 1990.

2. Blessed by the Past

Faithfulness to the tradition does not mean sacralization of the past, of the history of the church. Tradition is not a kind of immutable monster, a prison in which we would be confined for ever. It is a stream of life, driven and impregnated by the energies of the Holy Spirit, a stream which unavoidably carries historical, and therefore transitory, elements and even ashes and cinders. Sometimes it seems to stand still as if imprisoned in a layer of ice, but under the rigid frozen surface the clear waters of spring run. It is our task, with the help of God's mercy, to break through the ice, especially the ice in our slumbering frozen hearts... In us and from us, the tradition will become a spring of living water again. "From this ancient source", says a contemporary Orthodox spiritual father, "we will draw new strength."[1]

We were conscious as we met in Geneva in the autumn of 1992 that we were nearing the half-way mark of the time that had been designated the Decade of the Churches in Solidarity with Women. It may come as a surprise to some contemporary critics of the women's movement to learn that the earliest reference I can find to the church's standing in solidarity with women is dated around the year 150 A.D. It occurs in the writings of Tatian, an Assyrian who became a Christian in the second century, and who wrote an *Address to the Greeks*. In it he chastizes his correspondents for daring to slander the good name of Christian women. He reminds the Greeks that they are known to be disciples of women themselves, so they ought not to scoff at the women who participate in the Christian community, nor, as he puts it, "at the church who stands by them"!

Contrary to some modern assumptions, the Christian tradition is not inevitably sexist nor was it in its earliest days even implicitly so. As Kathleen Bliss pointed out in the first survey ever commissioned by the World Council of Churches, a report on the service and status of women, there is a veritable pageant of women who throughout church history have played key roles in the life and witness of the Christian community. To anyone who reads the New Testament with an open mind, it is obvious that it was bound to be so. Jesus came to bring good news for both women and men and there is no suggestion anywhere in his teaching that he regarded women as less holy or of less worth than their brothers. In the gospel stories themselves, women are by no means background figures, though the men who wrote the gospels give us tantalizingly few details about them. It is significant that in almost every case it is their deeds that are recorded rather than their words. One of them, the woman who anointed Christ with perfume, is immortalized by Jesus who commands that her story be told everywhere alongside his. Had she been a man, the gospel writers would no doubt have been rather more careful about recording her name and the church would surely have honoured her in some special way. Instead, she is consigned to that anonymity which is so often the fate of women. A group of women were constantly present in the company of Christ's disciples, though, in contrast to the detailed report of the calling of the men, we are given no account of how the women began their discipleship. It was to women that the first proclamations of Christ's coming were entrusted, at his conception and on the day of his resurrection, though on both occasions their announcements were greeted with scepticism by men. Charles Wesley celebrates this fact in one of his great hymns, though it is interesting to note that this particular verse has been omitted from all later editions!

> More courageous than the men
>   When Christ his breath resigned,
> Women first the grace obtain
>   Their living Lord to find;
> Women first the news proclaim,
>   Know his resurrection power,

Teach the apostles of the Lamb
Who lives to die no more.[2]

It was with women that Jesus had some of his most remarkable conversations. In these he praised their faith and engaged them in serious theological dialogue, often pushing their arguments out beyond the limits their conditioning had imposed upon them. But his disciples warned him of the danger of being seen too much in the company of women.

It is, then, from a theological rather than a historical point of view that we should note this special emphasis on the role of women in the gospels. We need to read not only the words that are written but seek to discover the truth that underlies them. The gospels are the foundation texts of our Christian tradition, demonstrating how the good news of the breaking in of the kingdom manifested itself. It is clear that the kingdom is an inclusive one, to which both women and men can have access. Their varied gifts are recognized. In their relationships with one another they are taught to show mutual respect.

At Pentecost a whole new community comes into being in which the Spirit falls alike on sons and daughters, and in which all the old distinctions between Jew and Greek, bond and free, male and female are to be done away with. A new "koinonia" is born, in which there is a common possession of the Spirit. The evidence in the book of Acts shows how that vision became a reality through the women whose names are recorded as leaders of the community, like Lydia, founder the church in Philippi, Phoebe, a deacon, Junia, an apostle, and the daughters of Philip who were recognized as prophets. But apparently, even in those earliest, heady days of women's liberation from their traditional roles of subservience and silence in the realm of religion, the men became anxious about their new freedom and in the epistles began to set limits on how far the women should allow the Spirit to take them. Yet women continued to exercise their ministry in the early church, as many catacomb paintings and early tomb inscriptions give evidence. There are paintings of women sharing a eucharist. There is an early tomb inscribed with the name of Leta, Presbyter. There is even in one church in Italy an early mosaic depicting Theodora, Episcopa. It has been argued that in each case these titles refer to a relationship — a woman who was the wife of a presbyter or one who was the mother of a bishop. Be that as it may — and many women have become used to being identified only through their relationships — there is no doubt that these women exercised a memorable leader-ship.

The women themselves seem to have set no limits to their courage in witnessing to their faith. Among the stories of the earliest Christian martyrs the names of women should be blazoned in gold, women whose amaz-ing steadfastness became an inspiration to the men who died with them. In one of the earliest accounts of the persecutions is the story of the slave girl Blandina. She was one of the martyrs of Lyons, put to death by the local Roman authorities out of superstitious fear of Christians. Blandina, we are told, had neither beauty nor rank but to her fellow sufferers she appeared like Christ himself:

> Blandina was hung on a post and exposed as wild bait for the wild animals that were let loose upon her. She seemed to hang there in the form of a cross, and by her fervent prayer she aroused intense enthusiasm in those who were undergoing their ordeal, for in their torment with their physical eyes they saw in the person of their sister Him who was crucified for them. [3]

A few years ago the sculptor Edwina Sandys caused an outrage when she sculpted the figure of a crucified woman as an image of Christ. Yet there could surely be no more appropriate memorial to those early women martyrs, and to all the women who throughout the centuries since have suffered torture and death for their faith, than to show how they too were crucified with their Lord. Among them was

the African noblewoman, Perpetua, who died in the persecution in Carthage in the third century. She kept a diary of
her sufferings. She wrote frankly of how frightened she
was when she was first put in prison, along with her baby
son whom she was breastfeeding. She prepared herself
and her companions for their ordeal by telling them of her
dreams, in which she saw a ladder leading up to heaven
and in which a shepherd brought her milk to drink. The
ladder symbolized that through martyrdom they would
ascend to heaven, and the milk recalled the drink given to
catechumens after baptism. She was accompanied into the
gladiators' arena by her slave Felicitas who had just given
birth to a child, and with dignity they faced their death
together.

The stories of such courageous women can be matched
in every century. They are part of what has been called
"the hidden tradition" of the church, the women who have
kept the faith and passed it on to succeeding generations.
Eager, like Anna in the gospel story (Luke 2:36-38), to
"go out and tell their neighbours", women have been
among the great apostles and teachers of the church. In the
Eastern Orthodox church, between the fourth and ninth
century, several women were ordained deacons and taught
in schools and congregations. Others attained wide reputa-
tions for their scholarship and piety. More than one of the
early ecumenical councils discussed and regulated the
work of women, demanding a high standard of theological
attainment among those who worked as teachers in the
church.

In every period of church history since, especially at
times when the Spirit has come sweeping down upon the
church again, disturbing it into renewal, women have
been caught up in its impetus. Despite the fact that in their
domestic life they were so often confined between the
walls of their own homes, in the world of the Spirit they
pushed out the walls of the church and claimed new
territories for the gospel. Many of the first converts to

Christianity in both the West and the East were women who opened doors to those who came as apostles to their own lands, like Queen Bertha who welcomed St Augustine to the shores of Britain, or the nun St Nina who paved the way for the founding of the Orthodox church in Georgia. In the establishing of the earliest religious communities, women were in the leadership, with abbesses being afforded a status of authority next to that of bishops. From the time of the Reformation onwards, women are found among those pioneering new ways of being the church. Among the Quakers, the Methodists, the Salvation Army and many similar movements, they were in the vanguard, exploring new avenues for the gospel, engaging in new forms of ministry and forming new patterns of partnership with men.

As the Western churches became stirred into a worldwide missionary endeavour, among the most intrepid of the pioneer missionaries were women. When missionary societies began to be formed, most of which excluded women from their policy-making committees, the women, undeterred, came together in their own associations to support their sisters overseas. It seems as though whenever a movement solidifies into a structure limits are imposed on women's ministries. But again and again throughout history women have gone on pushing out beyond the boundaries, refusing to become simply a solid, static base, supporting pyramids of male hierarchy.

So it has been with the ecumenical movement. In the earliest years of this century, when it was primarily a movement rather than an institution, women as well as men were actively involved in it. Through organizations such as the Young Women's Christian Association, the World Student Christian Federation, the Women's World Day of Prayer, women discovered their sisters across the boundaries of the denominations and worked together with their men colleagues in exploring new avenues of ecumenical experience. Yet when the expanding mission of the church led to the first world missionary conference in 1910, hardly any women were there in person, even though their presence within the missionary endeavour was very evident in the conference's agenda. An early recommendation of the ensuing International Missionary Council was that women should be afforded new opportunities for development and achievement. In 1923 plans were submitted for a study on the "Place of Women in the Church in the Mission Field". A questionnaire was sent to missionaries around the world, and a paper reporting on the response states: "We are not asking here for greater freedom or liberty for woman in these lands. She is demanding that for herself. What we ask is that... the church keep pace with the other agencies that are according her a new status and new opportunities for development and achievement... The church because of her own lack of vision is allowing trained, talented, spiritual women to slip away from her into other lines of activity."[4]

Similarly, the embryonic World Council of Churches initiated a study on the place and status of women in churches across the world, which revealed that women were showing great energy and enthusiasm for the new movement. Yet, as the World Council itself took institutional form and strove to involve the hierarchies of the churches, women became less visible in its midst and less influential in its policies. Though the Amsterdam assembly set up a special commission on the life and work of women in the church, even the boldly prophetic general secretary, Willem Visser 't Hooft, expressed some nervousness about the work of such a commission which, he said, would need an immense amount of tact in getting its ideas across.

Nevertheless, that commission, chaired by the distinguished Syrian Orthodox woman, Sarah Chakko, inspired a whole generation of women across the world, encouraging them to embark on ecumenical ventures. The first secretary of the commission was the English educationalist, Kathleen Bliss. It was she who, anonymously, had penned the memorable phrase that became the ringing message of the Amsterdam assembly: "We intend to stay together." The phrase applied equally to the women, who were beginning to form a new international network. Sarah Chakko took a long sabbatical year from her academic duties in India, devoting herself full-time to the work of the new commission. She travelled widely across the world, helping the women of the East and the West to listen to one another and to realize how much they had to share in their struggle to gain recognition in both church and society. In recognition of her leadership in the total ecumenical movement, she was eventually invited to fill a vacancy that occurred in the presidium of the World Council of Churches itself. So, in 1951, Sarah Chakko became the first woman president of the WCC, and gave outstanding leadership until her untimely death in 1954. Even so, the Council then waited almost twenty years before electing another woman. Dr Kiyoko T. Cho of Japan was elected between assemblies. Only at the Nairobi assembly in 1975 were women presidents voted to that office by the assembly itself.

There seems always to have been a fear that too much activity on the part of women would rock the ecumenical boat. Boats always are rocked by a wind, and maybe it has been the wind of the Spirit that has impelled women to go on making their presence felt with increasing force during this second half of the twentieth century. In each of the assemblies of the World Council of Churches a voice has been raised for women, increasing in volume at each successive assembly, as gradually they have managed to secure greater representation. It has not come about through tactful means alone, but through struggle and strategy, through special conferences and commissions and above all through the energy and unfaltering commitment of women on the ground floor of the churches on whom the whole structure still relies.

NOTES

[1] Elisabeth Behr-Sigel, "The Energizing Force of Tradition: Orthodox Tradition as a Resource for the Renewal of Women and Men in Community", in *The Community of Women and Men in the Church: The Sheffield Report*, ed. Constance F. Parvey, Geneva, WCC, 1983, p.62.
[2] From *Hymns and Poems on Holy Scripture — Unpublished Poetry of Charles Wesley*, Vol. II, ed. Kimbrough and Beckerlegge, Nashville, TN, Kingswood Books, 1990, p.207.
[3] Quoted in Karen Armstrong, *The Gospel According to Woman*, London, Elm Tree Books, 1986, p.173.
[4] Quoted in Susannah Herzel, *A Voice for Women*, Geneva, WCC, 1981, p.5.

3. Belonging Together

The moment we find it possible to set out from our different starting points on the "long journey" whose issue we know but can never see, we make a strange discovery. The way is really a stream which carries us forward, if only we take the risk of committing ourselves to it. We cannot restore paradise lost, but we can take the risk of entrusting ourselves to this living progress towards the kingdom of God, and find solidarity as we do so.[1]

Those of us who gathered in Geneva to share our memories and hopes of ecumenism carried in our own personal histories the story of the struggle of the past fifty years. It was notable that several of the women said how they had been present on the sidelines of great ecumenical gatherings, where, denied any official status, they had come into contact with other women from whom they caught the infection of an ecumenical enthusiasm. Others of us recalled how much we owed to those rare men who, contrary to the general practice in the churches, recognized our potential gifts and brought us into the wider ecumenical, international community. We were all agreed that what had kept us going was the sense of solidarity with other women embarked on the same pilgrimage. "Solidarity", as one of our members put it, "has become for us another word for koinonia", that sharing of things of the Spirit in a life of common experience which binds us together through a network of mutual support and understanding.

Three of the people in our group were now officially retired, but we were all as actively committed as we had ever been. Marie Assaad, of the Coptic Orthodox Church, had the longest ecumenical memory amongst us. She had gone as a YWCA delegate to the world conference of Christian youth in Oslo in 1947 where her enthusiasm was kindled into an ecumenical commitment that has lasted a life-time. But it was a long time before she had another opportunity to attend an assembly of the World Council of Churches. She and other women worked behind the scenes to ensure that the Coptic church sent delegates to the Evanston assembly. There Bishop Samuel became a member of the central committee where he served actively and effectively for the next twenty years until his own untimely death by assassination.

It was not until 1980 that Marie herself came into the structure of the WCC. At the invitation of Philip Potter, and in response to the strong instigation of many women, she was appointed a deputy general secretary. She confessed how unprepared she had felt for such responsibility. Coming from a church where women had never been a part of the hierarchy and having never had any formal theological training herself, she could not imagine what gifts she would be able to bring into a global ecumenical structure. She had been used to international recognition in the secular world, where her work in research on female circumcision had led her into active programmes to help eliminate the practice. She was also happily settled in Cairo where, although she was widowed and her children had left home, she had friends and grandchildren surrounding her. Going to Geneva would mean, as it has done for so many women, venturing out alone, becoming vulnerable in a male-dominated world and learning to allow God to use her in whatever way seemed most creative. Feeling literally small of stature in the midst of so many great and powerful men, she discovered in her new role that she was expected at first to conform to male stereotypes. There were occasions, she said, when even the sheer fact of her lack of height and her natural shyness meant that she felt excluded when men either failed to acknowledge her presence or spoke to her patronizingly, as to a little child. Despite her official status in the Council, some church leaders seemed quite unwilling to enter into any serious conversation with her or even hear her when she did venture to make any contribution to a discussion.

From that experience she learned three lessons important for women. One was to allow the Holy Spirit to
become a source of strength within us, giving us confi-
dence in our own God-given gifts. Another was to rely on
the support of other women who have to struggle against
the same kind of gender bias. It is important to check out
our ideas with them and ask whether they are as insignifi-
cant as some of the men seem to think. And thirdly, she
emphasized how important it is for women to stop being
apologetic about not having the same training and experience as men. Women sometimes apologize so much for
what they have not been given that they fail to realize the
strength of what they have to give. They need to believe
that they too have wisdom to bring that is deeply theological, in reflecting on what God is doing throughout the
whole of creation and particularly in the experience of
women.

A second ecumenical veteran among us was Marga
Bührig, whose memory went back to the Evanston assembly of 1954. Through the generosity of a friend, she went
there as a visitor, as what she called an "invisible
woman". But very visible to her at the assembly was
Madeleine Barot, of the WCC staff, the indefatigable
guardian of the concern for the co-operation of men and
women in the church. Through her persuasion Marga's
ecumenical pilgrimage began.

Back home in Switzerland Marga was for ten years the
director of a lay academy in Zurich. She was at that time
the only woman in a senior executive position of this kind
in German-speaking Switzerland and so had no models to
follow. Her predecessor had been a father-figure. She had
no particular wish to be a mother-figure, though some of
her male colleagues seemed to need just that. She had to
learn what it was like to have power, but was determined
to use it in a different way from the style most men
seemed to adopt. She was anxious not to be authoritarian
but to involve as many people as possible in the decision-

making that affected all their lives. It meant being open with everyone about what was happening and encouraging people, especially other women in lowlier positions on the staff, to discover gifts and abilities they had so far had no chance to develop. It even became necessary to develop a women's network of support to compensate for their exclusion from the "old boys' network" which operates in so many institutions! Marga said that she herself learned to survive in a world of male church politics through the support of close personal friendships, particularly of two women friends. She had welcomed also the opportunity of working in a team that included both women and men. She shared with them her vision that change must come from "below" and cannot be ordered or brought about by imposition from above. In various roles she was able to attend all the subsequent WCC assemblies, culminating to her astonishment in her election at Vancouver as one of the seven presidents of the World Council. She had never been particularly interested in the structures of ecumenism but was passionately committed to the movement. She hoped dearly that the World Council itself would learn some of the lessons about the importance of participation and partnership which she had learned painfully and slowly through the years.

I suppose I myself would count as the third veteran amongst us. My own ecumenical experience began at Uppsala in 1968, where I was one of those rare women then, a delegate in my own right sent by my own church. We women delegates made up only nine percent of the total number of official representatives. I vividly remember one woman delegate pointing out that in the local congregations, on whom all the churches depend, possibly ninety percent of the membership would be women. It was as a result of women at Uppsala pressing for greater representation in the central and executive committees that I found myself, to my great surprise, elected to both. I realized that this must have been hard at first for my own church to accept, as I displaced my church's senior official who had since the earliest days been our representative on the central committee, but he graciously gave place to me. I was even more astonished when I was elected as vice-chairman (as the office was known in those days). I realized that I had been chosen as a token woman rather than through any particular ability of my own, but I had to accept that in all humility. Often it was through tokenism at first that any of us women would be given the experience of working in committees, and through that experience might be enabled to push open doors of opportunity for other women. I remember being described in one article as a "figurehead of the ecumenical movement" which I thought a flattering description until I discovered the definition of a figurehead as a female figure with no functional role and only of decorative value! But at least from that position I hoped to be able to share in some way in steering the ecumenical ship into some yet uncharted waters. So I joined enthusiastically with Brigalia Bam, Madeleine Barot's successor at the women's desk, in planning a conference at Berlin in 1974 on sexism in the 1970s.

Sexism was a new word coming into the ecumenical vocabulary and many ribald comments were made about it at the time. Some even suggested that we had planned a conference on sexual activity in old age! But in effect the conference proved to be a landmark in the life of the WCC. It drew together a remarkably talented group of women from all over the world, who became motivated by a strong sense of the Spirit of God moving among us, impelling us to new determination to ensure a far greater participation of women at all levels of the church's life, including the councils of the WCC itself. A question that conference clearly answered was one that had been posed to me by one of the men on the WCC executive when we were arguing about the need for a greater presence of women in the committee itself (there were just two of us then). I had been challenged, in all earnestness, to say where we could find women of sufficient calibre to participate in an international and ecumenical gathering! The answer was right there before our eyes in Berlin — 170 of them from over fifty different countries, women whose experience as pastors and theologians, lawyers and politicians, doctors and economists, teachers and administrators, counsellors and home-makers provided a reservoir of talent and an abundance of gifts that the official ecumenical bodies had scarcely used until then.

The effects of that conference were plain to see even among our own small consultation meeting in Geneva eighteen years later. Three of the women present there — Hildegard Zumach of Germany, Sun Ai Lee-Park of Korea and Judy Monroe of the Bahamas — dated the beginning of their ecumenical awareness and, just as importantly, their consciousness of their vocation as women, back to that Berlin conference. Reading the list of participants now is like reading a roll-call of women from all parts of the world whose enormous talent has been committed to the ecumenical movement ever since. It was there that for the first time many women came to realize that the question of women's participation was not simply a matter of social justice, but of theological integrity. And it was there that many of us discovered the strength of sisterhood. We caught the mood of a banner on the wall which announced: "Sisters awake! Our time has come! Sisterhood is blooming. Springtime will never be the same again."

Philip Potter, who was at that time the general secretary of the World Council, came personally to address the Berlin conference. He stressed that it was not the growth of the secular women's movement that prompted the church's concern about sexism, but the gospel itself. The basis of the World Council's determination to address this issue was both theological and biblical. It was clearly revealed in scripture, he said, that God's purpose from the very beginning had been that men and women should, in their otherness, stand to each other in a relationship of companionship and complementarity. Yet ambivalence in working out what this meant for the Christian community had bedevilled the church throughout its history and still had not been worked out fully in the World Council itself.

At the Nairobi assembly the following year women were permitted to take over a whole session to explore the issue and present their case to the gathered company. They had so much to say that the session ran over time, but as one woman wryly remarked: "We have been silent in the Council for thirty years, surely we can be allowed an extra thirty minutes now!"

In the press gallery at Nairobi sat a young African reporter, Agnes Abuom, another member of our consultation in Geneva. She told us how eagerly she had listened to the debate and how moved she had been by the singing of the words that became the theme song of Nairobi, "Break down the walls that separate us". Later she joined the youth department of the WCC. She confessed that, working as a young, black woman in the Council she sometimes wondered what had happened to the freedom and unity we had talked about so much at Nairobi. She did not find even the ecumenical community free from patronizing prejudice nor eager for that co-operative partnership which can only be fully realized when women and men, young and old, black and white, learn to listen to one another and to reach out across the barriers of gender, age and race. Also from her experience in Geneva she had come to see the importance of solidarity with other women. Now back at home in Kenya working with the Anglican church, she finds that the women who are ordained and the many women in the laity of the church are discovering how much they need to give one another the support and strength to go further into an even greater partnership between clergy and laity as well as between men and women.

The study on the "Community of Women and Men in the Church", initiated by the Berlin conference and given the blessing of the Faith and Order Commission at its Accra meeting, had become at Nairobi an official study commended to the churches. The study guide became one of the most successful and widely used publications of the World Council. Over 65,000 copies were distributed, in numerous languages. It dealt not only with the question of women's present experience in the churches, but more importantly with a vision of what a truly ecumenical co-operation between women and men might become. The outstanding quality of the reports that came back was the theological depth of the issues they raised, but it was theology with a difference. The women hammered out their theology on the anvil of their experience, so it is no wonder that at times the sparks flew! But they were sparks of the Spirit. As the report based on the study, entitled "Towards a Fuller Community of Women and Men", puts it:

> No longer do we look *up* to bring *down* the Spirit — the life force — but *down*, then up from *down under*. Working out of pain, rather than out of sin, leads to a realistic dealing with pain as over against persistent suffering and guilt. Thus we free ourselves to live out of the solidarity in which we seek presence and grace for one another, out of which we connect with a past to recover women's history...[2]

So there began to emerge a theology that drew its inspiration from the context of the spiritual imagination as well as from cerebral concepts, and which recognized the validity of female experience as reflecting an image of God as clearly as male experience does. The study presented its findings in poems and stories and prayers as well as in reasoned argument, in cries of pain as much as in credal statements. It came to its culmination in the conference in Sheffield, UK, in 1981, which became another landmark for many women in their ecumenical journey. The members of the conference addressed a

"Letter to the Churches", presented at the central committee of the WCC meeting in Dresden. It spoke passionately of the "sighs too deep for words of women who suffer war, violence, poverty, exploitation and disparagement in a world so largely controlled by men". But it spoke positively too of a new vision for the future:

> We speak as those who have been seeking to listen anew to scripture and to live the tradition of the church in its many forms. Thus we have heard a word of God for today about a vision for our human life — a renewed community of women and men. We speak with urgency. In a world threatened by nuclear self-destruction women and men are made more sharply aware that they need a new partnership as equals before God; in churches and societies which men have dominated in ways deeply damaging to women and to men, we need both repentance and faith to move forward at God's call through the gospel... Sisters and brothers in Christ, we long that you will join us in giving reality to the vision which we have seen.[3]

Despite the eirenic terms in which it was expressed, the letter from Sheffield caused a ferment when it was presented at the central committee in Dresden in 1982. Once again, women were accused of rocking the ecumenical boat by daring to question both the direction in which it was heading and the crew which, literally speaking, were *manning* it! The request that the Council should work towards a fifty percent representation of women in all its assemblies and committees was treated as though it were extravagant and extreme. The very tentative questions raised about the ordination of women in some parts of the church across the world came to dominate the debate, whilst the much larger question about the subordination of women in almost all parts of the world was never seriously heard.

I can vividly remember one day during the central committee when we had been debating the controversial Programme to Combat Racism. It had won strong support

from many men who had experienced in their own lives
what racial oppression and discrimination meant. Later,
when we were discussing discrimination against women,
one of those same men commented to me over a cup of
coffee that this was simply a matter of culture and had no
relevance to theology! But the debate was clearly moving
on to theological ground and across the world feminist
theology has developed in many different cultural contexts. It is a theology that has grown out of the experience
of women in particular places, but it is also essentially
ecumenical, creating across the world networks of women
who share their experience, their insights and their sense
of community with one another.

That became evident at the Vancouver assembly,
where women made their presence strongly felt not only
as delegates but as speakers and leaders in all aspects of
the assembly's life. Before the assembly a preparatory
conference was held for women under the skilled leadership of Bärbel von Wartenberg who had by this time
inherited the women's desk at Geneva. She helped to
guide the women through the maze of an ecclesiastical
gathering of a kind few of them had so far had the
opportunity of experiencing. It introduced them to rules of
debate and procedure not always easy to grasp even by
seasoned ecclesiastical bureaucrats. They learned how to
identify items on the agenda which were of special concern to them and to prepare their own interventions. But
more important, it created among the women a strong
sense of belonging to a supportive community. We even
had our own haven to repair to when the going got rough
in the assembly itself, what became known as the "Well",
a place of refreshment provided for women by our hosts in
Vancouver. All this helped in the development of our
solidarity with one another. It is not surprising, nor
inappropriate, that when women who were at Vancouver
meet one another again, it is often the encounters at the
Well that they recall even more vividly than speeches at

the conference! It was after all at a well that Jesus engaged in one of his most searching theological dialogues.

So it seemed inevitable or, as the New Testament would put it, "right to the Holy Spirit and us" that the next stage of our ecumenical journey should be the declaration of the Decade of the Churches in Solidarity with Women, which began under the leadership of Anna Karin Hammar, while she was responsible in Geneva for continuing the concern for the greater co-operation of women and men. Leadership of the Decade then passed to her successor, Aruna Gnanadason, the convener of our Geneva consultation. I confess that the title of the Decade has always worried me, for it seems to suggest that there are "churches" on the one hand and women on the other, and that they still have not become fully integrated. It is rather like talking about children and young people as though they were "the church of tomorrow" when they are truly the church of today. But I realize that it reflects a sad reality in the life of the churches and an even more tragic reality in the life of the world, where so much of the burden of suffering in war-torn, famine-stricken or oppressed communities is borne by women.

It was their cry that we heard so poignantly at the Canberra assembly. That was the first assembly to express its theme in the form of a prayer rather than an affirmation. "Come, Holy Spirit — Renew the Whole Creation", we had yearned. In the agony of that assembly it was as though we could almost hear the groanings of that pregnant Spirit labouring to bring to birth a new creation. For some of the younger women present at our consultation in Geneva, it had been their first experience of a large ecumenical gathering, and they spoke in terms of pain as much as of joy, of despair as much as of hope. They had been shocked at the pressures women had been put under as they tried to gain full acceptance as representatives of their churches on the policy-making bodies of the Council. They had found many of the procedures alienating to women. Some had even experienced sexual harassment or simple disparagement. But for all of us who were there at Canberra, the abiding image had become that of the woman holding in her hand a torch of fire, an appropriate symbol of that Spirit that has led God's faithful people through the centuries and had brought us thus far on our ecumenical pilgrimage.

But where do we go from here? That was the question we were to address in our consultation.

NOTES

[1] Liselotte Nold, "None of Us Returns Home the Woman She Was When She Came", in *Sexism in the 1970s: Discrimination against Women*, Geneva, WCC, 1975, p.132.
[2] Quoted in Susannah Herzel, *A Voice for Women*, Geneva, WCC, 1981, p.107.
[3] "A Letter from Sheffield", quoted in *The Community of Women and Men in the Church*, ed. Constance F. Parvey, Geneva, WCC, 1983, pp.91-93.

4. Beginning at the Base

It will take more than a decade to discover how God is making all things new, but for the present we can all participate together in a decade of midwifery and childbirth... The waters are being troubled and some of the gifts of that troubling are the way the Spirit is raising up new sons and daughters to dream dreams and see new visions.

Across the world today there is a new ecumenical ferment at work. Up from the grassroots and mass movements, and out of the universities and the labour unions is coming the internationalization of the women's movement. These linkages are part of the hope for rebirth in the churches; a hope already upon us in the small signs of the Spirit as it troubles the water. [1]

We had introduced ourselves to one another at the Geneva consultation in the customary way in ecumenical gatherings. We presented our credentials by referring to the WCC assemblies we had been privileged to attend (albeit in most cases only on the sidelines) or the central committees or commissions to which we had, as a result of considerable pressure, eventually been appointed. But our meeting sprang into life when we began talking about our experiences in the places where we live and work. There we are caught up in hurricanes of upheaval howling across our world, shaking the structures of our societies to their foundations, crushing many lives in their wake, impelling us to find new ways of responding to the human need we see all around us. Ecumenism becomes then no voluntary option. We are impelled towards one another as the spirit of compassion constrains us to work together in the face of issues that have become matters of life and death.

For Judy Monroe, who had come to our meeting directly from the Bahamas, such imagery was no mere rhetoric. The island of Eleuthera only a few weeks before had been hit by a fierce hurricane. Judy described how structures of steel had become entangled like spaghetti and the homes of poorer people had been swept away as debris. She drew one memorable lesson from all this. There had been no hurricane in that area since 1929, so people were quite unprepared for the devastation that so suddenly swept down upon their peaceful island. Though they had heard of storms in other parts of the world, they had rested in the kind of complacency that says: "If it's not happening to us, we don't need to prepare against it." Judy saw one of the functions of a global organization like the World Council of Churches to be that of making people aware of what is happening in other parts of the world and as concerned about it as if it were happening to members of their own family. Through her own ecumenical experience she had been enabled to develop this kind of global awareness, which has stood her in good stead in the responsibilities she has since been given in her own professional life. Elected as the first woman president of the chamber of commerce in the Bahamas, she felt she must try to put her experience in the business world at the disposal of the worldwide ecumenical community. The most rewarding period of her life, she said, had been her years as the first woman president of the Ecumenical Development Co-operative Society, an organization that encourages investment in small, co-operative ventures in the poorer parts of the world. Like so many women who become the first in a position of responsibility, she was able to open up the way for another woman to succeed her. The EDCS venture has become now a true partnership of women and men, in which policy is made by joint decisions between those who have capital to invest and those engaged on the projects that need investment.

The image of the hurricane was one that aptly applied to the situation in Germany today, as both Hildegard Zumach and Margot Kässmann testified. The euphoria of the days when the Berlin Wall was first broken down has evaporated into a more sober realization that the intense nationalism that once prevailed in Germany has by no means crumbled away. Recent racist attacks, perpetrated mainly by men, but supported in some cases by women, has sent shock waves through the nation. This has led to great demonstrations of men and women from all parts of society coming together in attempts to counteract the vicious fear of the foreigner. As one who grew up in Nazi times, Hildegard spoke of how it was through the ecumenical movement that she had caught the vision of racial harmony and human unity that has inspired her whole life. She was among the women in Germany who had organized the boycott of South African fruits, which had at first alienated the institutional church, and later alerted it, as to what was happening under apartheid.

The idea for the boycott had first begun in the Black Women's Federation in South Africa, who had spoken to German women about their plight under apartheid. When that Federation was banned the German women decided they must become in their own church and community the voice of their silenced sisters. So they organized a boycott of South African fruit. The purpose was not only to exert economic pressure on South Africa, but to alert the public conscience in Germany as to what was going on there. So groups of women came out of their homes and took to the streets. There they put up information stalls, produced street theatre, and played music in the market place. The bishops thought the campaign ill-advised as it might alienate people and cause controversy in the church, but the women persisted, saying that they were acting out of love for their African sisters and brothers, which required them to work for justice. It became for them a witness to their faith. They kept a regular vigil for African political prisoners right in front of the South African embassy, and they attended shareholders meetings to ask about companies' and banks' involvement in South Africa. Through taking part in the boycott the women themselves were changed. They met many critics in the church, and many friends outside it, but above all they found a sense of solidarity among themselves and a sense of supporting and standing alongside their sisters in South Africa.

Now, said Hildegard, there needed to be a similar active resistance to the growing racism at home and a more effective witness among the churches to the breaking down of all walls of partition, between races, nations and sexes alike.

Aiko Carter had come to our consultation from her desk in the National Christian Council of Japan. There, twelve years ago, she had been given responsibility particularly for so-called "women's concerns". What were those concerns envisaged to be? The fiftieth anniversary of women's ordination had already been celebrated in the United Church of Japan. It had come about not through any conviction about the special gift of ministry that women had to bring, but simply through the emergency situation created when the military government of 1941 had insisted on a reorganization of all religious institutions. This required increasing the number of pastors, so women were brought in to fill in the gaps. The negative result was that women were not encouraged to make any specifically feminine contribution, but to model themselves on men, even negating their own sexuality and resolving to live celibate lives lest family responsibility interrupt their pastoral responsibilities.

It was in the secular world that Aiko found a greater awareness of what really are "women's concerns". This was so particularly in the peace movement which followed the testing of more H-bombs in the Pacific area. Hearing of the terrible effects the fall-out from such radiation was having on unborn babies and on their mothers, women of all faiths and none joined together in protest, carrying banners demanding "A future for children" and "No more Hiroshima". Such peace movements gained support from women across the world who saw this working for peace as their most urgent priority. Aiko told us how she herself had gained the courage to confront the authorities by meeting with other women in the worldwide community. After attending the Vancouver assembly as an interpreter she went to share in the Hiroshima Day protests in Tahiti. There she was arrested by the French authorities who wanted to see all her notebooks. But as they were written in Japanese, her captors were unable to read them! So she was released. Nowadays, she said, many Japanese women are gaining courage through their contacts with women from other parts of Asia in their campaign for peace. Do we not hear in all this too the fluttering of the wings of the Spirit, the dove of peace?

Another of the "women's concerns" that soon became evident to Aiko was the desperate plight of young Thai women who had come to Japan in search of some means of survival and who had finished up selling themselves in the bars and brothels of Tokyo. One woman who tried to escape was brought by the police to the Women's Christian Temperance Union for housing. But there was no one who could speak her language or knew how to deal with her. On the third night she left quietly after having written a note which was later translated as saying: "Why was I born into this unfortunate life and sold to work in Japan? Now I can never go back to Thailand which is so far away. I am punished with the sin of this life." Out of her need came the establishing of a HELP community (House in Emergency of Love and Peace), where women are working together in welcoming those who have lost all their self-respect. Sharing in such a community, women of many different backgrounds are helped to recover a sense of their own worth and find mutual support.

A similar centre in Korea is described in the magazine *In God's Image*, which is published by the Asian Women's Resource Centre for Culture and Theology. Sun Ai Lee-Park is the editor. She explained that, in this ecumenical body, culture as well as theology comes into the title out of the realization of how much the two are intertwined. Asia has a great wealth of religions of all kinds, and all of them have both liberative and oppressive elements as far as women are concerned. But in Korea few of them have shown much awareness of the appalling exploitation of women in, for example, the rapidly growing international trade in prostitution. Too often the churches turn a blind eye to the tragic suffering of millions of young Asian girls, some of them only children, who are forced to resort to this degrading way of earning money for their families. In the magazine a Korean woman pastor writes of her work among these oppressed women, seeing them as Jesus saw them, not as potential converts, but as friends who have much experience to share and who, in discussing their problems with one another, become themselves the basis of a caring, compassionate community. The pastor tells movingly of how, when she herself was planning to go home to visit her family for the full moon festival, she asked the girls whether they were going home too. "We dare not," they said. They had been abandoned by their families and in any case they were ashamed to go home. After that, the pastor herself has never left for a home visit during holidays. Instead, she stays to cook with the prostitutes and celebrate the festival with them.

I have often wondered myself why prostitution is so often regarded as though it were mainly a "women's concern", rather than an outrage against the whole of our humanity. I remember reading once of a press conference convened in the Philippines in an attempt to expose to the world's media the facts of this growing "industry" in what is known as sex tourism. The majority of the male journalists present seemed to think it was not an issue of urgent interest. After all, prostitution, they said, is the oldest trade in the world and in many countries people turn a blind eye to it. Yet the Christian community in this, as in so many issues concerning women, has a mandate from Christ himself to protest against such degradation and to befriend and respect those who are the victims of it.

It is through working among the oppressed in this way and through active participation in movements like the peace campaigns that women in Asia are rethinking and reformulating their theology, as they meet the Christ who, in the words of the Asian theologian Kosuke Koyama, "has gone to the periphery". "'Going to the periphery' as Christ did", Dr Koyama has said, "makes a person a theologian."[2]

That same vision of what it means to take one's ecumenical commitment out beyond the boundaries was shared by Annathaie Abayasekera who had come to the consultation from war-torn Sri Lanka. As a former member of both the WCC executive committee and of the commission of the Programme to Combat Racism, she was no stranger to official ecumenism. But it became real, she said, when it became local. Her present ambition is to mobilize women in the pews to a much greater awareness of the need for concerted action within their own country. She herself has often been under personal threat because of her stance on human rights in Sri Lanka and through her work amongst the women whose labour is exploited in the tea plantations. At one time she was even arrested under the anti-terrorism act. She wondered whether she might in fact just "disappear" as many have done. But it was at this point that she came to understand the meaning of solidarity. The women's network stepped in and kept up a campaign for her release. This was not a group that was restricted to the church. One of the women, a Hindu lawyer, told Annathaie: "While you were detained, some of the women met together many times, and felt that this was the community you really belonged to and we must do something to help you." Through that experience she had learned that the community is the company of people with whom we are broken in the struggle. That community includes many people who are in the churches, but it is far wider than the church itself.

Recently, groups of women in the Church of Sri Lanka have cut across the denominational barriers and come together to study the Bible, affirming one another as they do so and trying to work out what they can do to help bring an end to the tragic violence that is tearing their land apart. In a historic event they organized a gathering of theologically trained and well-informed women from different ethnic and religious backgrounds to address the special needs of women in the long-drawn-out civil war still raging in the island. Similar efforts are also undertaken by groups like Mothers and Daughters.

It is, after all, women who so often have to bear the brunt of violence, whether it be in the aftermath of war or even within what might have been thought of as the shelter of their own homes. Annathaie feels deeply the need for the churches as a whole to recognize that the so-called "women's issues" are urgent issues of justice and need to be taken far more seriously in all the councils, synods and day-to-day pastoral work of the church. Too often the church's response to a woman who is the victim, for example, of domestic violence is merely to point out to her the importance of her marital vows. Even a pastor may fail to discern her pain and see how the very image of God is being distorted within her. Yet in all parts of the world women are prey to this kind of physical, sexual or verbal violence even in their own homes, where it is too often cloaked in silence.

As we went around the table telling the stories of women we knew and what was happening to them in the places where we live, it was as though we were listening to a variety of voices singing the same song, the song of women coming together to empower one another and to discover their united strength. Aruna Gnanadason said that her years working with the women's movement in India and being associated with the Centre for Development and Women's Studies in Madras had been the richest ecumenical experience of her life. She had been part of a women's group which campaigns to end all forms of violence against women. One particular concern was what is known in India as "custodial rape", i.e. rape that takes place in police stations or other institutions. The women were originally alerted to this issue in the mid-1970s by an incident of grave injustice. A fourteen-year-old girl was raped in a police station by two policemen. The Maharashtra high court indicted the policemen. However, the supreme court reversed the judgment, saying that there was not enough circumstantial evidence to prove that the girl had not consented to intercourse. Women all over India organized around the demand that the case be reopened. This led to a demand for a change in the more than a century-old law regarding rape. From this forum against rape, the movement grew to include various other forms of violence against women: the image of women in the media; the exploitation of women's labour and sexuality; the harm done to women's bodies through the abuse of medical technology, particularly in matters related to the reproductive process; invasive contraceptive devices; the practice of using amniocentesis to detect and subsequently destroy an unwanted female foetus. The Centre aims to empower women themselves to challenge such oppression and provides legal and counselling services to those who are the victims of it. Such situations are literally matters of life and death.

The ecumenical movement, as Aruna put it, should be present at the bleeding points of the world, where so often it is women who bleed the most. But there is a new awakening. Referring to the struggle of the Dalit people in India, Aruna said it was as though those who had once accepted their lot as "no people", who must remain invisible at all costs, are gaining visibility as "new people" whose full human dignity must now be recognized.

"Trying to make women visible" was how Louise Tappa, a Baptist pastor from Cameroon, described her own vision of an ecumenical movement which would encourage a much more active role for both women and young people. That vision had been partly realized recently when over 7,000 people, the majority of them women, had come from all over the country to celebrate the day when she herself had been ordained to the ministry of the word and sacraments. They came from all denominations, many of them bringing their menfolk with them. Some wondered how a woman, and a single woman at that, could cope with such a task, which they had only seen done by a man. But Louise had reminded them: "I am ordained, not by men, but by God." Part of her work is in a rescue centre for girls who have become lost in the life of the city. "Some people call them drop-outs," she said, "but I prefer to think of them as those who have been squeezed out." The centre had been founded and was managed entirely by women.

From Africa also, Agnes Abuom spoke about how the ecumenical movement could be a sign of hope for women, pointing the way ahead not only for the churches but in civic and political life too, where there are still too many hindrances blocking the road to their full participation. It is sometimes forgotten that in the struggles for liberation, women played an important role, just as in the church they are the strength of the laity. Yet neither in church nor state is that contribution fully recognized. Women still have to rely on other women to give them the courage to go on.

Her words echoed for me those of a miner's wife in Yorkshire in the north of England. For years she had silently accepted her role as a mere appendage of her husband. Then, in the recent struggles of the miners to preserve their jobs and to defend a whole way of life in the mining villages, she and other women had joined forces in support of their husbands, and even more important, in a discovery of their own strength. "Once," she said, "I was only somebody's something — daughter, wife, mother — but now at last I am somebody." "Nothing hits the heart", said another woman engaged in the same struggle, "like fighting for a community. It really hits home. It isn't about money or getting people into power. It's about being together and caring for one another."

That, it seemed to me, was not a bad definition of the ecumenical movement, though I doubt whether that miner's wife would even know the word! It expresses the kind of new-found strength and solidarity that women are discovering across the world. There are networks of communication between women which are not always formal nor even verbally expressed. Sometimes it is through silent protest that women make their presence felt as they demonstrate for human rights; sometimes it is through brightly coloured collages or quilts that they depict the creative power of those who work together to make something beautiful; sometimes it is through their singing or dancing that they express the harmony of those who share their hopes.

It is that kind of vision and imagination that women are bringing into the ecumenical movement. There is a kind of subversive "gossiping" going on among women all over the world, still telling the story of one who came to put down the mighty from their seats and to exalt the humble and meek. In my own church in north London when, in an ecumenical Bible study, we were discussing the Magnificat, a Jamaican woman commented: "When I hear those words it makes me feel great." That was a good colloquial translation, I felt, expressing exactly how Mary felt when she first sang: "My soul does magnify the Lord, for He that is mighty has magnified me!" It will only be when we can sing that song together, women and men, and have learned to magnify rather than to diminish one another, that the new order will really have begun. Only then shall we bear a full witness to our many-splendoured gospel, a gospel that is meant not just for women, nor principally for men, but for women and men together and for the whole creation, the oikoumene of God.

NOTES

[1] "The Spirit Is Troubling the Water. Ecumenical Decade: Churches in Solidarity with Women", in *To the Wind of God's Spirit: Reflections on the Canberra Theme*, compiled by Emilio Castro, Geneva, WCC Publications, 1990, p.102.

[2] Kosuke Koyama, "Jesus Christ Who Has Gone to the Utter Periphery", in *The Ecumenical Review*, vol. 43, no. 1, January 1991, p.101.

5. Storming the Bastions

An oikoumene of women is not the same thing as women in the oikoumene. The deeper significance of our efforts for the quotas was to bring women into the ecumenical movement. We wanted women to be there, just as we wanted young people, representatives of oppressed groups, handicapped people and other categories to be there. Women in the ecumenical movement are women who have made ecumenical history — the women who have defended the women's cause with courage and tenacity. Today we are in the process of taking the next step. The oikoumene of women is a worldwide community of women, active in many fields, who are engaged in altering the face of the world and of the ecumenical movement.[1]

Despite the fact that the voices of women have grown stronger throughout the world, and their capacity for leadership is no longer in doubt, they are still often heard in the churches as a threat rather than a promise, and they have not yet been able to make their full impact upon the whole ecumenical community. It is true that there are more women now in the various councils and committees, but our striving to ensure their presence there was never meant to be an end in itself. What we long to see is a community in which women feel that the theological reflection growing out of their experience as women will be allowed to share in shaping the church of the future as much as the wisdom of men has done in the past. As women, we care as much about the church our grandchildren will inherit as we do for the church we inherited from our grandparents. That is why we long so much and pray so earnestly for its unity. That is why we believe too that it must have the freedom to move where the Spirit blows. And that is why we feel so strongly that the ecumenical movement must never become so captive to the ecclesiastical institutions that it cannot enlarge the boundaries of its community and explore new frontiers in its mission.

Some of our group had worked in church-based institutions, and they shared with us something of how what once seemed rigid structures are now in fact beginning to yield to the Spirit's pressure. Bertrice Wood from the USA was herself a former student of the graduate school at Bossey, and was for many years a consultant to the Sub-unit on Women within the structure of the World Council of Churches. Her experience in both these situations, and particularly working alongside Brigalia Bam, had raised her awareness of all that women could accomplish in ministry and in working together towards the unity of the churches if they were given the chance. Having served since then as moderator of the women's commission of the WCC, Bertrice has more recently returned to theological study. There she found that many of the students, like herself, were women embarking on a second career and turning with eager interest to the study of theology, but in many cases it is a theology that has grown out of an experience of pain or rejection or downright oppression.

Bertrice herself has been teaching a course on ecumenism, trying to help her students to see how the quest for the unity of the church is a vital and urgent part of the quest for the unity of the whole of humanity. Yet it sometimes seems, in official ecumenical circles, as though the concerns of women are regarded as leading to disunity. In the Message of the Primates of the Most Holy Orthodox Churches given at Phanar in March 1992, special mention is made of two serious obstacles to the unity of the church — the ordination of women and the use of inclusive language in reference to God. It is almost as though women are held hostage to the commitment to a certain ecclesiology. They seem to have, as it were, their hands tied behind their backs when it comes to discussions like the subject of the ordination of women, lest it cause offence to those churches for which the concept is alien to their tradition. Yet ecumenism must surely mean that we can learn to live together in one faith even with those from whom we may profoundly differ on matters of order.

Bertrice is now working on a doctoral dissertation entitled "Towards an Ecclesiology of Ecumenism". Her special focus is directed to what is known as the Toronto statement of 1950 which defined the relationship between the World Council and its member churches. It had emphasized the purely consultative nature of the ecumenical body, and recognized that churches may differ fundamentally in their concepts of the church. Yet it agreed that they must be willing to work together in trying to discern the mind of Christ and to assist one another through mutual instruction, help and renewal. This statement has been regarded as a milestone in the life of the World Council. Bertrice, like many others, wonders whether it may not now be something of a stumbling block too, in the sense that it sets limits as to how far churches are prepared to venture in fellowship along with those from which they differ on some fundamental questions. This could seriously inhibit those who feel that they are being led by the Spirit into new ways of ministry and of doing theology as they seek to respond to the many changes sweeping across both the churches and the world. It could prevent the ecumenical family from discovering what it means to belong to a community that is truly one, in which women and men share in the partnership of the gospel.

One of the striking features of church life today is the steep increase in the number of women now studying theology in seminaries in all parts of the world. Particularly active are the women members of the Ecumenical Association of Third World Theologians. They have themselves held several regional consultations in which Asian, African and Latin American women have been able to reflect together on how their theology is shaped by their experience of working with women who in many cases are the poorest of the world's poor so far as material possessions go but are among the richest in their spiritual resources and strength. Out of their reflections have come profound insights which need to be shared with the whole church, and not just with women. In the introduction to a book entitled *With Passion and Compassion*, a group of third-world women theologians have written:

> As one reads of women's lives in the church, the evidence begins to emerge that "women become dangerous" when we question "the powerful and masculine model of the internal structures of the church", and as such our presence has been construed as a source of tension. The mark of faith and hope and love is that through all this, women together strive to find new paths to become effective partners in the church, impelled by the love of Christ demonstrated not only on the cross but also in the affirmation of women's bodies and of our full humanity. Women's relationship to the church is founded on their Christology.[2]

Yet "filling the holes" was how Ofelia Ortega described the role of women as once seen by the church in Cuba. After the revolution, when Cuba was denuded of any missionary presence and all the institutions founded by the missions needed staffing, Ofelia found herself ordained as the first woman pastor in Cuba and immediately appointed as the director of Christian education. She was regarded as a "strong woman" capable of taking on several jobs at once — home-making, studying and doing her pastoral work. She warned other women against being known as strong. It is possibly wiser to let people see your own vulnerability. Eventually she had the good fortune to come as a student to Bossey, a portent of what lay ahead, for twenty years later she was appointed to the staff there, a job she now combines with her responsibilities for ecumenical theological education.

Ofelia's concern about theological education comes out of her own experience when she, as a young woman, earnestly wanted to be involved in the mission and witness of the church. But it took a long time to convince others that it was worth training a woman as a theologian.

Surely, they thought, she would be happier as a pastor's wife or a children's teacher or a worker in a church office.

It was in the secular world of community work that Ofelia felt herself affirmed as a woman and began to discover something of her own strength. Sharing in literacy campaigns throughout the countryside, she came to realize how liberating a force education can be as it releases within women gifts they never knew they had. She came to feel that within the church a woman's potential is too often anaesthetized. Spirituality tends to become identified with the domestic virtues of humility and selfless devotion to one's family rather than with determination to develop one's gifts and to participate fully in the life of a wider community. "For us women," Ofelia once wrote in an article describing her own spiritual journey, "the movement to maturity includes not only finding our independence but also belonging. Acceptance, relationship, belonging are all crucial elements in our spiritual journey."

Jeanne Becher's experience of ecumenism has been mainly located in the life of the staff at the Ecumenical Centre itself. There her special concern for women's issues had led sometimes to painful clashes with some of the men in the house, even on one occasion to a "sit-in" by women colleagues at a meeting of the Staff Executive Group. That was at the time when the programme of the Canberra assembly was being planned, where the hope was that women would play a major part throughout the assembly, and not just be relegated to one special session of their own. It was through encounters of this kind, Jeanne said, that she felt women themselves had grown in self-understanding and in solidarity. Now, many of the men on the staff had come to realize that the concerns of the women were their concerns too. The new structure of the Council has meant that issues once regarded as matters for the women's desk alone are dispersed throughout the house and shared with all other related departments. But

Jeanne's greatest inspiration still came from her travels out from the Centre. In Asia, Africa and Latin America she had met groups of rural women who showed enormous spiritual strength as they tackled the daunting struggle to survive. Since our meeting in Geneva, Jeanne, Aruna and Margot have all been members of the ecumenical team which travelled to the former Yugoslavia in response to the reports of systematic mass rape, abuse and suffering of women in the context of the fighting there. They went to listen to the women themselves, and to make their voices heard across the world, as they challenge churches and women's groups to acts of solidarity with these victims of such horrendous war crimes.

Such solidarity is one of the fundamental purposes of the ecumenical movement and is often the only hope for people whose voices would otherwise go unheeded in the powerful places of today's world. Barbara Stephens bore testimony to that as she told how a new, all-embracing ecumenical body had been formed recently in Aotearoa-New Zealand. Even so simple a gesture as using that name for her country, she explained, is a way of acknowledging the treaty made with the Maori people by the settler government. At first the new ecumenical body appointed three women in the general secretariat, but that had lasted only for three years. It seemed that ecumenism with a female face was unacceptable to many in the churches. To be authentically recognized, a church body was still expected to have male leadership. So alongside there grew up a meeting of male church leaders, presumably to provide the authority and status it was felt the body needed. Yet within the conference there were people, women and men together, who were trying to work with new models of leadership which did not depend on the old hierarchies. They were particularly trying to establish a partnership with the Maori people in a movement which would eventually be able to bring together the two different cultures in Aotearoa-New Zealand and to reach out more fully to the rest of the Pacific region in which they are located.

Perhaps one of the best definitions of ecumenism came from Mercy Oduyoye who suggested that the ecumenical movement has become for her a kind of family tree, where the relationships are not of flesh and blood but of those bound together in the Spirit, sharing a common concern about what God is doing in the world. She said she had first learned to look to other women for support, not in the church but during her years in the university. She had been dismayed by the kind of prejudice still found against women even in such a supposedly enlightened place. When she herself left the university to come to take up a senior post in Geneva, some of her male colleagues suggested that it was a bad example for her to set to other African women, who ought rather to be encouraged to stay at home with their families. "The only type of family life which some African men will allow is what their grandmothers knew," Mercy said. When previously she had worked for the WCC, she had been on the staff of the youth department. There she had frequently to ask: "Where are the young people?" Now working as deputy general secretary she has almost as frequently to ask: "Where are the women?" This is an even more abiding concern for, as Mercy wryly observed, though she has ceased being young now, she will never cease being a woman!

NOTE

[1] Reinhild Traitler, "An Oikoumene of Women?", in *The Ecumenical Review*, vol. 40, no. 2, April 1988, p.184.
[2] Eds Virginia Fabella and Mercy Amba Oduyoye, Maryknoll, NY, Orbis, 1988.

6. Beyond the Boundaries

We must together seek the fullness of Christian unity. We need for this purpose every member of the Christian family, of Eastern and Western tradition, ancient churches and younger churches, men and women, young and old, of every race and every nation. Our brethren in Christ are given to us, not chosen by us. In some things our convictions do not yet permit us to act together, but we have made progress in giving content to the unity we seek. Let us therefore find out the things which in each place we can do together now; and faithfully do them, praying and working always for that fuller unity which Christ wills for his church.[1]

Half way through our consultation, we were shown a draft study guide that had been produced by a group similar to ours, meeting in the same week but including men and women together. It suggested that in working towards a common understanding and vision of the future of the World Council of Churches, we should address ourselves to three issues in particular. We should consider how the WCC can contribute to the unity of the churches; how it can help the churches in their vocation; and how it can develop relationships within and beyond the World Council of Churches.

On all these three issues we were asked to give our distinctive insights as women. The unity which women have found in working, praying and worshipping together both within and beyond the community of faith has given us a holy impatience with the continued divisions within our splintered churches. One of the longest-established and most widely-observed ecumenical events within the life of the churches has for over a century been the Women's World Day of Prayer. In several parts of the world it is the only service in which Orthodox women join with their Catholic and Protestant sisters for a service of prayer which women themselves prepare, sharing the concerns of women in various parts of the world and incorporating some of the riches of our various spiritual traditions. In official ecumenical circles this great event can still pass almost unnoticed, but for many women it is their most memorable experience of the unity of the church. It makes it all the more tragic that in countries like Northern Ireland and South Africa ecclesiastical or racial barriers still keep sisters apart from one another even on the World Day of Prayer.

Another rich experience of ecumenism which many of the women in our group described was the growth of what is known as "Woman Church". The term was first used in a conference organized by a coalition of Roman Catholic groups advocating the renewal of the church and the greater participation of women in all parts of its life. Today, in many parts of the world, women who belong to different churches but who feel excluded often by the language of the liturgy and the predominantly male leadership of their own churches use the term to describe a new kind of ecclesial fellowship they have found with one another and with men who feel the pain of women's exclusion. They find their spiritual home in small communities which transcend the denominational divisions and enable them to express in worship the feminine experience, seeking to discern what it means to believe that women too are made in the image of God. Some who belong to "Woman Church" remain at the same time faithful members of the institutional churches, hoping that one day the creative, inclusive and holistic liturgies they develop in "Woman Church" may eventually enrich the life of the whole Christian community. Describing one such "Woman Church", the St Hilda's community in London, Monica Furlong has written in an introduction to their book of services and prayers:

> We wanted men as well as women to be an integral part
> of the community because part of what we wanted to learn

and to teach the church was a more equal and generous way of gender-relating than any of the churches (even those which already ordained women) seemed to understand. We wanted a community that worked by consensus and not by hierarchy. We wanted to call the new group a community, not because we would be living together but because we wanted to share — gifts, ideas, leadership, vision and perhaps sometimes possessions and money. We wanted it to embrace anyone who came to it, and our earliest rule was that anyone who came to a liturgy was part of the community while they were visiting us.[2]

We were not suggesting that any of the manifestations of unity as we women have known them should give rise to a separate "oikoumene of women", but we do urge that the movements towards greater unity in the churches catch up with the insights and experience of women in these local groups. They can show the churches how inclusive authentic ecumenism must become. After all, as Bärbel von Wartenberg-Potter has put it: "What kind of unity will it be if it is achieved without the agreement of women?" So far, in most of the bilateral church conversations, or panels negotiating church union, women have been included as little more than a token presence. We urge that their insights are needed, not just because they are women but because so much of feminine theology and experience can open up new horizons of what it means to be the church in its mission to the world today. We believe that women could point to new ways of being the church in its conciliar form, a body that does not depend upon the dominant leadership of any one group, but allows all to contribute until consensus can be reached. If on some issues that proves impossible, then at least everyone will have been heard and their views respected even if it means that in the end the community has to hold in tension differences of viewpoint and of understanding. In a consensus model there are no winners and losers, only sharers in a common search for truth.

This way of working would demand of the churches a stronger commitment to one another and to the World Council itself. So long as the churches feel no obligation to act on decisions taken in meetings of the Council, nor to report its deliberations to their own communities, nor to give any priority to its programmes, there is bound to be paralysis in the ecumenical movement. Some of our members who had been at the Seoul conference on "Justice, Peace and the Integrity of Creation" in 1990 suggested that the term "covenant" was helpful in describing the relationship of the churches to one another and to the Council. It is after all a biblical and an ecumenical term. At its heart is the call of God which is both promise and challenge: "I will be your God and you shall be my people." On the one hand, the people promise to obey God's commandments; on the other, they find themselves belonging together to a new community. When the World Council was formed in 1948, it described the churches as "covenanting" to stay together. The same term is used in parts of the world today where there are local ecumenical projects between churches which have not yet come into any formal unity, but which have been compelled to work together by the very circumstances surrounding them. "Covenanting" is seen as an expression of their determination to grow together and act as far as possible as if that unity were already God's gift to them.

Such churches seem rather like couples who are seen in one another's company so much that one is tempted to ask them: "When do you intend to marry?" They may reply: "Oh no, it's nothing like that, we're just good friends!" Yet it is clear that they are being driven together by a love they cannot resist. So does the love of Christ constrain us towards a greater unity than we have been prepared yet to explore.

When we are asked what we see as the vocation of the ecumenical movement as we approach a new century, we would say that it is to call the churches out to new frontiers in the struggle to manifest God's rule over the earth. It means prompting the prophetic voice of the church to cry out in the wastelands of our modern world that the time has come for women and men alike to repent and to believe the good news that is meant for all people, without exclusion. That will mean the ecumenical movement allying itself not only with the institutional churches but with all those other movements which struggle against the principalities and powers that would deface God's image and destroy God's creation.

Movements like the recently formed SISTER (Sisters in Struggle to Eliminate Racism) have brought women together across the frontiers of the nations and the boundaries of the faiths. It was organized from two desks in the World Council of Churches now working together in the Programme Unit on Justice, Peace and Creation: Women under Racism and the Churches in Solidarity with Women. It recognized that women, who often suffer from multiple oppression, find their strength in this kind of global solidarity, which organizations like the World Council can do so much to facilitate and develop. But to have the resources for that kind of vocation the movement needs the institution. So movements must become a constant challenge to the churches to recognize and to respond to that need.

Such response requires a fostering of relationships not only between the churches and the councils, but also between the churches and the movements. It was after all from the movements that the whole ecumenical movement received its first impetus. That is why we wondered whether it would not be possible to open up more entry-points into the ecumenical circle than simply through the denominations. In Aotearoa-New Zealand, for example, the constitution of the new ecumenical body includes not only representatives of the member churches, but delegations from different parts of the constituency — young people, for instance — and ecumenical delegations from different regions of the country. Now there is growing discussion to include so-called "marginalized" groups. Thus does the ecumenical circle continually enlarge its circumference, keeping clear its central focus on the One who holds all things together.

We thought there was a danger that sometimes the World Council of Churches is seen as a kind of ecclesiastical version of the United Nations, where all its delegates sit as representatives of their own nation's or denomination's point of view. Some of them give that impression when they make their pre-prepared speeches on issues that affect their particular region. We felt that a council of churches needs to have much greater freedom than that, freedom to move at the behest of the Holy Spirit. People need ears to listen more attentively to one another, eyes to see things from a different perspective, and hearts ready to respond to the visions and dreams of others who share in the koinonia, the common possession of the Spirit. A council should therefore be a place where people are enabled to transcend their national and denominational divisions by being exposed to those movements and even those other faiths across the world through which the Spirit of God may well be wanting to give us new insights and call us into new paths of obedience.

Yet at the same time we could see that it is not only from a worldwide perspective that we can discern God's will. The gospel that was proclaimed and enacted by Jesus in a particular place at a particular period of history is a gospel that has taken root in many different soils and been nurtured in many different cultures. One of the most enriching theological developments of the past few years has been the theology that has arisen in those different contexts and out of those different experiences. Those regional and contextual approaches must somehow be brought together and be enabled to contribute to the development of our whole ecumenical theology. Among them much more serious attention needs to be paid to the increasingly perceptive feminist theology, which places great emphasis on the need to foster relationships of caring and nurture between people at all levels of life. Such theology draws its resources not so much from libraries as from the many wells across the world where women meet together in their search for the living water that can sustain their souls.

That may take us beyond even the boundaries of our faith as we know it today. Many of us as women have found our sense of solidarity extending not only to those who share our own faith but also to women of other faiths and even to those who have given up any formal expression of faith at all but who, in this increasingly materialistic world, are still seekers after spiritual truth. Several of us have attended at various times interfaith meetings of women and have been profoundly moved to hear our sisters sharing so many of the same experiences as we have encountered in our own faith community. In many cases they felt as we did that they had been taught to read their scriptures through the eyes of men, to observe the traditions according to the dictates of men and to participate, or not to participate, in rituals as prescribed by men. And yet they too, as they have dug more deeply into the mine of spirituality out of which their faith has been hewn, have discovered hidden treasures of women's devotion, of women's mysticism, of women's wisdom and of women's faithfulness in keeping faith alive through centuries of persecution and oppression. As we have shared these traditions with one another we have all felt our own faith enriched and our ecumenical vision enlarged. It has taken us beyond dialogue, listening and speaking to one another in humility and openness, and on into acting together as allies in the common causes of caring for God's creation, striving for justice for God's children, and seeking that peace which is God's will for each of us and for all the peoples of the world.

As some of us discovered at the meeting with guests from other faiths held in Mauritius prior to the Vancouver

54

assembly, "the world today is most deeply divided, not between religions, but between those in each religious tradition who hold their faith in a narrow and exclusive way, and those in each tradition who hold their faith in a generous and open-handed way".[3]

In a world where all the major conflicts have their roots in some religious discord, and where for many people their very survival can depend on living in peaceful co-existence with neighbours of different faiths, it has become more vital then ever that "faith should speak peace to faith". This for us has become "the new ecumenism".

NOTES

[1] "The Message of the Assembly to the Churches", *The New Delhi Report: The Third Assembly of the World Council of Churches, 1961*, London, SCM, 1962, pp.321-322.

[2] Monica Furlong, *Liturgy for an Agape: Women Included*, London, SPCK, 1991, p.6.

[3] Diana Eck, "Inter-Religious Dialogue as a Christian Ecumenical Concern", in *The Ecumenical Review*, vol. 37, no. 4, p.417.

7. Baptized in Tears

> In baptism the old and unjust relationships among classes, castes, races, ethnic groups and genders cease to exist. They are drowned in the water of baptism. And if they are not, can we still recognize the church, the new community in Jesus Christ?[1]

It was not surprising that in a company of women, the image of baptism as a new birth was one that brought vivid memories. In our group were several women who were not only committed ecumenists, active in their local communities or in the various councils of the ecumenical movement. They were also, as they proudly displayed in photographs exchanged over the meal tables, mothers or even grandmothers, who had themselves given birth to a new generation. In fact, Margot Kässmann summed up her life concerns as coming under three headings. In German it used to be said that women should keep to three areas of responsibility, known as the three K's: Kinder (children), Kuche (kitchen) and Kirche (church). Margot offered her own updated version of that formula as the three C's in English: children, church and the conciliar process! In her life all the concerns seem to be intertwined. During the last ten years, in between attending assemblies and central committees of the World Council of Churches, she has given birth to four children, as well as continuing her theological work at a lay academy.

It was the experience of giving birth that had given her new insight into what is meant by the whole symbolism of baptism. She had found that as soon as a pregnant woman feels the waters break within her, it is as though her body is taken over by an enormous power that compels the new life to come out into the world, for it is no longer protected in the mother's womb. When it does emerge, smeared as it is in blood and sweat, it is in that moment that the mother, taking the vulnerable little life into her arms for the first time, feels the closest relationship of all. There are tears, the mother's mingled tears of exhaustion and joy, and the baby's tears of shock as her lungs breathe in for the first time the cold air of an alien world. Then the baby is washed in clean water and clothed and laid in a cot, and her life as a new, separate individual has begun. Now she is given her own name and brought to church, to be bathed in the waters of baptism, symbol of a new birth and of being received into the protection of a new community. So she begins to make new relationships, with her father and siblings, her grand-parents and godparents, and her larger family, the congre-gation of all God's people.

This is the community into which we are born, not by flesh and blood but by water and the Spirit. It is a commu-nity in which the baby is no longer defined primarily by her genetic inheritance, her race, her abilities or her gender. She is simply accepted by grace as a child of God. How *dis*-graceful it is that we live in a world where still in many cultures the girl-child is less valued than the boy. In many societies it is he who is more likely to inherit the wealth and to carry on the family name, whilst she is thought of as eventually being "given away" into another family. But no one can take away her baptismal name nor the value marked upon her brow with the sign of the cross. The family of God, through baptism, does away with all discrimination.

We were given other vivid images of the meaning of baptism in our sharing of experience in the group. Aiko Carter told the story of a "peace walk" that had taken many women to Okinawa, a battle-ground of the second world war. Many Koreans had been killed there, and stones collected from Korea had been built into a huge monument in Okinawa to commemorate the dead. The women gathered there, as Aiko put it, "to listen to the stones". One of the Korean women stood by the stones weeping. It was like keeping vigil in the Garden of Gethsemane. Then she gathered her tears in her hands and baptized the others with them, sharing her pain and bidding them: "Go forth into the world in peace." Having told us the story, it was typical of an Asian woman that she wanted to share with us a gift too. Aiko sent round the table to each one of us a tiny, paper dove, and for a moment we paused from our talking to ponder in our hearts on the pain of women the world over who are left weeping after the wars of men.

In a volume of *The Ecumenical Review*, one of our number, Marga Bührig, had written an article on that important phrase in the basis of the WCC which refers to the fellowship of the churches as a community of those "seeking to fulfill together their common calling". In that article she probed what we mean by that word "together". How often do people feel that they are included in full participation in the very sacraments of the church? As illustration, she told the story of a baptism she once attended in a basic community in Rome:

> [It was] a service in an ordinary room in a working-class district, close to the homes and work places of the people attending it. In the centre of the room a large table, festively laid with flowers, bread and wine, water for a baptism. Hymns simple enough for everyone to sing; a text from the gospel, a short meditation, some testimonies of the members' personal experience on the subject of the text, which concerned marriage. Then came the baptism of the child, with the words of baptism spoken in unison by the whole congregation, while the act of baptism itself was performed by a priest. Then anyone in the congregation who wanted to do so could express their wishes for the child and its parents. Everyone felt free to do so. Last came the celebration of the eucharist, bread and wine shared by everyone and, after that, a cheerful picnic in one of Rome's parks. Everyone had brought something along, everyone shared everything. I was there as a guest along with an ecumenical group and I found the experience unforgettable. This was real sharing of life; worship and everyday life were not kept separate from one another. Yet the leader and founder of this group had been excommunicated by his church...[2]

My own most vivid memory of a baptism is of one that took place in Geneva, within the fellowship of a World Council of Churches' consultation. It proved to be an eventful occasion, the first meeting of the commission of the Programme to Combat Racism, which was later to cause so much controversy within the ecumenical family. It began with worship, and it was a service which included the baptism of Ann Grace, the three-week old daughter of one of our commissioners, Joyce Clague, an Aborigine from Australia. Her husband, Colin, originally of Manx origin (the people of the Isle of Man, one of the ancient, original communities of Britain), had come with her to look after the baby while she attended the meetings. The whole commission gathered for the service. We were a mixed group both racially and by gender. I found it significant that the commission of PCR was one that never had any problem about recruiting women. Women are so often in the vanguard of the struggle against racism that they obviously had to be part of our membership. We were mixed too in our religious allegiance. One of our consultants, who asked if he might attend the service, was a Muslim. Philip Potter led us with a meditation about the meaning of baptism as acknowledging the "pre-venient grace of God", which covers every child coming into the world. As he held in his arms that tiny girl, born out of the love of two people of different races, who carried in their histories the memories of bitter oppression and long struggles for recognition, he called us to commit ourselves to work for the kind of community where Ann Grace could grow up into a world of acceptance and of hope. That was over twenty years ago, and the need for that kind of commitment, especially so far as the treatment of aboriginal peoples is concerned, is as urgent as it ever was.

Baptism is a sign both of our unity in the church and the unity of all humanity. One of the most recent ecumenical churches to be built in Britain has the most striking baptistry I have ever seen. The church is called the Church of Christ the Cornerstone, and it has been built by all the churches together in one of England's newest cities, Milton Keynes. Emphasizing its community life, it is circular in shape, centring around a baptistry for those who want adult baptism and there is a font beside it for the baptism of infants. A stream of living water flows over them both, bringing the promise of the cleansing of the church for the refreshing of the world.

NOTES

[1] *Women in a Changing World*, no. 29, August 1990, p.25.
[2] Marga Bührig, "Seeking to Fulfill Together", in *The Ecumenical Review*, vol. 37, no. 2, April 1985, p.204.

8. Breaking Bread

As women bake bread and share it with their families,
I break my bread to share with you.

In God's new world we share the Bread of Life.

As women shed their blood to give you life,
I shed my blood to give you a new life.

In God's new world we share the Wine of Heaven.[1]

I was once asked by my Jewish neighbour why no women ever appear in pictures of the last supper. She said that no Jew would fail to honour his mother if she were present for such an important meal. I could only reply that I imagined that the women who accompanied the disciples to Jerusalem had been busy baking the bread, laying the table and fetching the water so that the men could wash their feet! Then it occurred to me how significant it was that Jesus took over the servant role from them. He became as it were one of them, and rebuked his disciples for not valuing servanthood above leadership.

It is strange how often, in discussions about women's changing role in the world and in the church, we find ourselves accused of wanting power. Men rarely seem to analyze what it means that they have power. They may be critical of the way power is used politically or in the realm of economics, but they rarely seem aware of how they use it in the church. It sometimes appears as though styles of management they have seen in the secular world are taken over into the life of the church as well. Status and ceremony, efficiency and the control of finances, outlining goals and evaluating achievements may be in danger of becoming more important than the cherishing of relationships, particularly with those who have the least power of all.

In choosing a meal table as the great gathering place of the Christian community, Jesus was surely showing how those who break bread and pour wine together are brought into a relationship where all share both power and weakness, both strength and vulnerability. As the bread is broken and the wine is poured, we commemorate all whose bodies are broken in the struggle for their humanity and whose blood is shed in order that others might have life.

Perhaps that is why some of the women at our consultation told of the impact upon them when they first received the eucharist at the hands of a woman. One described how a woman pastor she met did not, as the traditional male practice is, serve herself first but, like a mother feeding her family, gave food and drink to everyone else before she took any for herself. Another spoke of how much more personal the service seemed to become as the minister spoke to each one directly, naming them as she gave them the elements. Again, I seemed to hear echoes of the gospel narrative as it describes how Jesus presided over that last supper. Yet we were fully aware that the eucharist is more than a family meal (though it surely ought not to be less). It is a celebration of a community found in communion with one another and with God. If there is no true community, there is nothing to celebrate.

There were some among us who felt that no one should be excluded from such a celebration. We were told of Asian women bringing their babies and feeding them with some of the communion bread, of a three-year old bringing her playmates and asking to be allowed to come to the party, of a whole African village wanting to share the meal together and of guests from other churches or even of other faiths requesting that they too might share in the feast.

As in the whole church, even in our small group we were divided on the question of whether there should be any fences put around that holy table. We respected those who see the eucharist as a sacrament of unity itself so that it would be false to suggest that that unity exists whilst we are still so divided. We are a broken and a hurt community. Until those hurts can be healed and we find a way of becoming fully reconciled to one another, some feel we cannot come to the altar together. There we so re-enact the drama of Christ's passion that we dare not pretend that we have already healed the wounds. But there were others among us who felt that it is only by coming to the altar together that we shall come to realize what it means to be truly a part of that one body broken by our sins, sharing in that blood shed for the sins of the world.

There was much discussion among us of the impatience some of us feel now at the slowness of the progress towards full communion. The older ones could see how the ecumenical movement has in fact brought us closer to being at the Lord's table together. At recent assemblies we have rejoiced in the great celebrations of the ecumenical liturgy that came out of the Faith and Order commission meeting in Lima in 1982. It is a liturgy that marks the achievement of an impressive consensus on the joint understanding of baptism, eucharist and ministry in the church. But therefore it is all the more sad that still there are large parts of our community unable to share fully in such a eucharist, a fact which makes us feel more keenly the pain of our divisions. There is a sense in which we want both to honour the tradition of the church and at the same time transcend it. Yet, as one of our number commented, we are like those who cry out to God in despair: "When shall we have this unity?" And it almost seems as though God's response is: "Not in my life-time!"

In the meantime, there are other celebrations we can enjoy together. Many of us have enjoyed the revival of an old tradition of "love-feast", an agape meal, where we share simple food together, tell our stories, give our testimonies to one another and recall the many times when Jesus was recognized by his friends as he broke bread with them. There is a poignancy in this linking of sharing food with the expression of our response to Christ's love for us all. In an article on women and Christology, Mercy once gave a graphic description of how closely Christ and food are linked in the minds of the poor:

> When an African woman walks ten kilometres to the source of water, there she finds the Christ waiting and thirsty as Jesus of Nazareth was on the cross. When African women sit in refugee camps with people they are unable to feed, they understand what it means to see the crowd and have only five loaves and two fishes — how they wish the sands of the Sahara could be turned into cornflour! Faced with the struggle for political power among men, the African woman shares with the Christ the view that to be great is to do the serving — for the Christ came to serve. The Christ is the companion of women whose broken body is given for us. As African women sit in the smoke of wood fires, or grill fish on coal fires, they prepare to give of their labour even before they are asked — theirs is a labour of love such as Jesus performed on the shore after his resurrection... The question raised by Christology and mission as lived by African women is this: "Can women's approach become a leaven to leaven the whole community or is it to be taken for granted as being what is expected of women?"[2]

Every meal can become a symbol of Christ's call to us to share our bread not only with one another, but also with the hungry multitudes in our world as we strive to live in imitation of Christ himself. It is this brokenness, between those who have and those who have not, between the rich and the poor, between the starving and the overfed, which should choke our conscience as we come to the table of the Lord. This is the division that is the real scandal that should bring us to our knees in shame and penitence. No wonder that as we pray "Give us this day our daily bread", Christ has bidden us to go on immediately to say "and forgive us our debts as we forgive those who are in debt to us".

Every shared meal can become a model of our ministry to one another. Sun Ai Lee told us how even a simple meal served after a church service became that kind of model in her own parish in Korea. One Sunday the pastor, her husband, suggested that the men should do the washing up of the dishes. This suggestion was resisted even by some of the women, saying it was below the dignity of men. But the pastor went into the kitchen himself until gradually the other men went to help him. Now the church has become known as "a church where men wash dishes", an astonishing concept in a Korean context!

Following that story, several of us started to recall incidents where a man has shown a willingness to learn from a woman or has been willing to give place to her, so that she might be free to exercise gifts of leadership and he might learn more of the privilege of service. We heard of partnerships in team ministry in which new patterns of pastoral care were emerging as men and women worked side by side. There is hardly any reference to this kind of experience in the documents on baptism, eucharist and ministry. We felt that more models of different styles of ministry were needed as we look into the future mission of the church. It seemed to us too that there has to be a much greater emphasis on the role of the laity, both men and women. So often they are the people who are out on the frontiers of mission confronting a world where the struggle is to keep any faith at all.

Yet we felt that often people who want to play any role in the church are expected to conform to all the traditional ways, to repeat the prescribed creeds and to fit in with the clericalized, hierarchical systems that have grown up over the centuries. We wondered what place there is for those who want to question the old ways and have difficulties with some of the ancient formulations of belief. In a world of the growing strength of fundamentalism in all the faiths, we felt there was a danger that women particularly become vulnerable to a dogmatic approach that tells them it is a virtue to keep silent rather than to ask questions and to be submissive rather than assertive. But many women today are wanting to explore new ways of doing theology that reflect on their own experience. They want to be heard as well as to listen, they want to be recognized as people with gifts to bring and love to express. They want to be doers of the gospel and not hearers only. Yet they find themselves trapped into ways of thinking and acting that are alien to their feminine experience. As one of the younger women in our consultation said: "To have any influence at all in the councils of the church, I have had to learn how to play the political games and speak the ecclesiastical language, but sometimes I feel as though I'm sitting next to myself while I'm doing it!"

Most women are more concerned about people than about processes or even programmes. We would like to see the World Council of Churches facilitating the meeting of people with others whom they would normally never have the chance to know. Instead of so many centralized consultations we would recommend that there be greater numbers of teams travelling to share in the everyday life of the faithful men and women who make up the local communities that week by week share in the communion of the body of Christ. In encounters of that kind people can be encouraged to go beyond the limits of their own experience and enter into the lives and concerns of their sisters and brothers in other parts of the world.

Bertrice gave us a moving illustration of such an experience happening to her on a visit to Romania. She had grown up in a tradition of worship which prides itself on its simplicity. So she had reacted strongly against any kind of iconography. But on a festival day she was invited to attend the liturgy. There came a point in the service when the people moved forward to kiss the icons. "That", she thought stubbornly, "I am not going to do." But a nun nearby beckoned to her and took her hand. What should she do? Risk offending the nun, or offend her own conscience by kissing the icon? She decided the relationship with her new friend was more important than her old scruples. So she went forward to kiss the icon, and burst into tears as a whole new experience of reverence overwhelmed her. In that moment, she realized that through the nun the Spirit had helped her to go a step beyond in her own spiritual journey.

NOTES

[1] Monica Furlong, *Liturgy for an Agape: Women Included*, London, SPCK, 1991, p.64.
[2] Mercy Oduyoye, "Alive to What God Is Doing", in *The Ecumenical Review*, vol. 41, no. 2, April 1989, p.199.

9. Braving the Journey

> What we can and must learn from the women who have started the trail-blazing is that feminism does offer a way forward, a way of healing our dangerous divisions and a way back to the Christian truth of service, equality, justice and the renunciation of power through love. It is possible; it is only in a vision of that possibility that we can hope to have the courage to set out. [1]

For many years after the first world war, 11 November was observed in Britain as Armistice Day. It was a time for commemoration of the men who died on the battlefields fighting to defend their country's freedom. In more recent years the memorial part of the observance has moved to the first Sunday in November. But there has always remained something sombre about the actual day, especially when, as it usually is in the West at that time of year, the weather is cold and the days are short. But in Britain 11 November 1992 has become a day to remember for a different reason altogether. It was a day on which some mourned but many more rejoiced; some saw it as a day of ecumenical gloom, others as a new dawn of hope for the whole church throughout the world.

It was the day on which the synod of the Church of England met for the decisive debate about the ordination of women to the priesthood. It was the culmination of many years of agonising arguments, some based on scriptural grounds, others holding to the traditional orders of the ancient church. Some women were pleading that the Spirit of God was doing a new thing and that in many churches across the world their sisters were now free to respond to a call to the ministry of word and sacraments. The debate was long and serious. Uppermost in its concerns was the ecumenical effect of whatever decision should be made. Whichever way the vote went, people would be hurt, some relationships would be damaged. But for many the very credibility of the gospel was at stake.

Does the church have good news for women as well as for men? Is the gospel a liberating or a confining force? In a Britain that is now largely secularized this particular debate received more media coverage than any other ecclesiastical occasion. For once, the world was listening to what the church had to say.

Throughout the day the microphones and cameras were present, relaying to a bemused radio and television audience all the arguments, some of which to an eaves-dropper must have sounded arcane. But the television cameras caught one image which no one could misread. Three young women deacons were sitting in the public gallery, listening to every word as intently as if their very lives depended on it. The elder statesmen of the church and some of the women on the floor of the debate swayed the synod first in one direction and then in another. Then the archbishop of Canterbury rose to speak. He admitted that the church was on the verge of making a great venture of faith. There were ecumenical risks attached to it. But after much prayer and searching of the scriptures, consultation with other churches and conversation with men and women of differing views, he had himself reached the conclusion that the time had now come when the church must be ready to receive those women whom God was evidently calling into the priesthood.

When eventually the time came for the vote, which had to attain a two-thirds majority in each of the houses — of bishops, of clergy and of laity — it was still not clear which way the decision would go. In a prayerfully quiet gathering the archbishop stood to announce the result. All three houses had agreed to go forward to the step of ordaining women in the Church of England. The television cameras immediately swung up to those three young women in the gallery, hugging one another in a rapture of joy, tears running down their faces, like captives who have just heard the pronouncement of their freedom. Now at last they were free to obey the compulsive call of the Spirit within them. Outside Church House, in the gathering gloom of evening, a forest of candles blazed into light as men and women who had been keeping all vigil all day broke into singing and cheering and dancing in the streets. It was like the song of the psalmist: "When the Lord turned again the captivity of Zion, we were like them that dream. Then was our mouth filled with laughter and our tongue with singing. Then said they among the heathen, the Lord hath done great things for them" (Ps. 126).

I record this incident in some detail, though it happened a few weeks after our consultation in Geneva, because it illustrated for me so well the ambiguity forced upon us by our ecumenical commitment and the risk that is involved whenever we feel called to a new venture of faith. In our consultation on the future of the World Council of Churches we had deliberately not made the ordination of women one of our major topics, though most of us realize how integral that debate is to the whole question of the role of an ecumenical body in future years. We cannot for ever avoid from our agenda every topic which might offend some of its members, particularly one which raises fundamental questions about how we view the whole of womanhood. If women for some reason or other are incapable of being an icon of Christ or of handling the sacred elements, then fundamental questions about Christology and about sexuality too need to be faced. We must ask what it means to say that in Christ we all become a new creation and that women as well as men can be carriers of the Spirit. We cannot stay sheltered in the static ark of ecumenism whilst the Spirit wings her way out beyond the storms, beckoning us to new horizons.

Equally important from the point of view of the theme of this book, we must ask what we mean by ecumenism. There were many references made in the Anglican debate to the holy catholic church. In the ecumenical movement we still have not clarified which churches are included within the embrace of that term. Our ecclesiology still needs much clearer definition if we are fully to recognize all the members churches of the Council as being catholic in the true sense of the word, and as striving to be holy under the guidance of the Spirit. We are all part of a pilgrim people who are still far from reaching the goal of our journey.

Considerations like this led the members of our consultation, when they came to sharing their dreams of the future, to hope that we would be prepared to take far more risks in the coming years. Our relationships with one another as churches should by now have reached that kind of maturity that enables us to speak the truth in love to one another. We should also be more prepared to believe that the Spirit will guide the whole church into all truth, even if at times she seems to reveal glimpses of it to different parts of the church at different stages of the journey. So often in the past spiritual renewal has seemed to threaten schism.

My own church, once known as "the people called Methodists", began as a renewal movement within the Church of England. But the Church of England could not contain it. Eventually division became inevitable and for a hundred years the separation widened into a great gulf. Much has been done in this century towards bridging that gulf. We have even tried structurally to bring about a scheme of reunion. Some seemed to think we were constructing a coffin and others a cradle. Perhaps we were doing both. Death and birth are parts of the same process, and each initially is an experience of separation. But both we believe are stages on a journey to a new life. We too, for many years, out of ecumenical considerations, refrained from taking unilateral action on the ordination of women, saying it was a gift we wanted to share with the whole church after we had rediscovered our unity. But the unity never came. Despite considerable theological convergence the two churches could not agree to walk together on a path of reconciliation. So we in the Methodist church became free to follow the prompting of the Spirit which we had felt for a long time, and for over twenty years now we have been blessed by the ministry of women.

We found ourselves in our consultation wondering where we women will have reached in our journey of faith as we come to the end of this decade of solidarity, an event which incidentally will coincide with the silver jubilee of the World Council of Churches in 1998. Will the assembly of that year have heard all that we have been trying to say to the churches during this past decade? Some feared that it is turning out to be a decade of solidarity of women with women, largely ignored by the rest of the church. It was even suggested that some women show greater solidarity with one another when they are together than when they are in the presence of men. Some even thought we might need a "Decade of Men in Solidarity with Women" or, if not a decade, at least a conference similar to the sexism conference of 1974, but this time organized mainly for men, to raise their awareness and aid their liberation from their gender-bound roles.

But we looked forward too to the day when no such special decades are necessary any longer, when we really shall experience the liberation that belongs to the whole of humanity. We long to see the ecumenical movement, in whatever form it takes in the future, being totally inclusive of all who come. That means being inclusive in the language that is used, in its ways of working, in the very form of its structures. We long to see the ecumenical councils giving a model to the churches of what it means to be a community that enables all who belong to it to feel that they can participate in its whole life, its worship, its decision-making, its mission in the world. That could mean that the World Council should cease to be too concerned about its success and its survival and become more prepared to make mistakes and even through them to find a revival of the Spirit. We would like it to be a council where no one's concerns are trivialized or laughed at, but where we begin to find that those concerns which once were furthest from us become closest to us. We would like to learn how to celebrate that which brings joy to others and not to engage in a kind of hierarchy of suffering ("I suffer more than you do!"). We want to see the World Council enabling the churches to recognize how interconnected and indeed how international are all the issues of our time. There are no specifically "women's issues", or "matters concerning young people", or "third-world problems". We are all in the same boat and our concern is for a journey in which we can all travel together towards that goal that is defined for us as the new heaven and the new earth. We want to see a greater care for the earth and for the whole of God's creation and for the churches to be engaged totally in the struggle to establish peace with justice on the earth. We long for a community where we can so accept each other that none need feel threatened in such a way that he or she feels the need to devalue others.

We realized as we shared these dreams that they might sound utopian, but those of us who have been in the struggle for these things for many years hold on to that hope and want to pass it on to another generation.

Our last word was a more modest one. Marie Assaad reminded us that for Egyptians like herself the end of a decade is a very short time. They are used to thinking in terms of millennia. But at least our prayer must be that through the decade of solidarity more men and women will have learnt to affirm one another and to listen to one another and that through the World Council of Churches this might have a ripple effect throughout the whole world.

NOTE

[1] Sara Maitland, *A Map of the New Country*, London, Routledge & Kegan Paul, 1983, p.194.

Envoy

A stone is thrown
into a calm lake
and the stone makes waves
spreading, reaching to the far side.

Let us throw stones into the deadly calm
of the lake that is our world,
no matter how small
is the stone,
no matter how small is the wave.

The stone brings awakening,
the wave is a movement,
and the movement spreads
when all of us
standing together on all sides
around the lake
keep throwing
our little stones.
The wave will never cease
till the whole lake
starts bubbling with life.

Extract from a poem by
SUN AI LEE-PARK